Eugene G Harfield

Commercial Directory of the Jews of the United Kingdom

Eugene G Harfield

Commercial Directory of the Jews of the United Kingdom

ISBN/EAN: 9783337129590

Printed in Europe, USA, Canada, Australia, Japan

Cover: Foto ©ninafisch / pixelio.de

More available books at **www.hansebooks.com**

A

COMMERCIAL DIRECTORY

OF THE

JEWS

OF THE

UNITED KINGDOM.

BY

G. EUGENE HARFIELD,

Author of

"THE PAST FROM A FUTURE STANDPOINT,"
"AN ORIENTAL CONSTELLATION,"
"EL ANSE," ETC.

LONDON AND RICHMOND, U.S.A.
HEWLETT & PIERCE.
—
5654 : 1894.

ENTERED AT STATIONERS' HALL, LONDON,

IN THE

YEAR 1894,

BY

G. EUGENE HARFIELD.

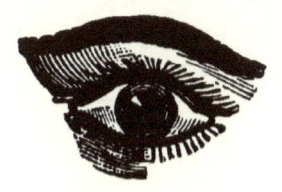

TO HEAVEN'S WILL

AND

PALESTINE'S FUTURE

I HUMBLY DEDICATE

THIS VOLUME.

INTRODUCTION.

The utility of the directory as a medium for consultation, both in a business and general manner, is too well known to require special comment by way of introduction here. That such a compilation of any particular sect or class selected from a country's inhabitants—apart from its creedal statistics and ceremonies—is at all requisite, or, to say the least, judicious, must be certainly negatived, in as much as they constitute a part of the whole of that country's population, responsible alike for its progression and contributing equally towards the maintenance of its dignity. To reduce, for instance, to certain statistical environment the Puritan, or Quaker class as in contradistinction to the Wesleyan, or Protestant, or Dissenter; that is to say, that to enumerate, define and to publish their several individual pursuits or

INTRODUCTION.

collective financial status as an exemplar of exceptional prosperity where civil and religious liberty is a safeguard to persecution, even annoyance, would be not only to enter a disclaimer to the established principles of freedom, but to demur at the introduction of liberty itself. The fact of class-distinction *per se*—apart from spiritual tendency—would at once proclaim desirability for severance from the body politic and invite enviable comparison, the hot-bed of contention and avarice, open the gates of the dark ages that have so firmly been barred since the close of the fourteenth century, and revive the wearing of the stigmatised " Rouelle " enacted by the so-called " Saint " Louis of France and Pope " Innocent " III. at what was known as " The Council of Lateran," in the middle of the thirteenth century.

Yet though such inconsistency might be objectionable, even unpardonable, in any national branch, forming, as it does, an actual part of the national tree, no such charge could be laid at the door of the Jewish race, being a nation of itself, unconnected genealogically with any other, either by admixture or grafting; and however much we may commingle socially or in mercantility; or, as is our pleasurable duty, give to that country in which we severally dwell our patriotic devotion, we are still an individual people, and in the introduction of such a compilation disloyal to no tutelary power. That such a publication is at all necessary cannot be even personally affirmed

INTRODUCTION.

at first glance, and it must be admitted, however reluctantly, that its inception by the editor, is but the result of a pardonable desire for novelty the permissibility for the assumption of the which history furnishes many a precedent and to which even many an important city owed its origin and many an empire its downfall. And, who knows, but this, the first of its kind in the history of Directories, may prove conducive, in a measure, to some beneficial result.

Among many other allegations of Russia, exclusive of its sectarian objectiveness, is that of the uselessness of the Jewish subjects on the ground that they confine themselves to a few chosen trades only, thereby contributing but little to the country's credit. The list of trades and professions and various mercantile pursuits in the hands of the Jews of this country, at once the most extensive and flourishing realmdom under the sun, yet the most tolerant, and where perfect freedom is accorded all dogmatical dissentients with a most lavish hand, tend to dispel any blame that may be attached to them on that account, by reason of restriction and proscription there.

Bah! it is the old story of envy and avarice of the indolent spendthrift towards the thrifty, integral economist! Not alone is the result of their frugality kept under constant surveillance by the "green-eyed monster" but the simplicity and purity of their lives form a continual reproach to their licentiousness!

INTRODUCTION.

History teems with such records in every age and clime and among all nationalities and creeds, though it has been the misfortune of Israel to suffer most, as much because of their steadfast adherence to national characteristics as to the state of enervatedness born of incessant attrition and remembrance of forfeited grandeur; bowing in contrite submission to the chastening will that exiled them their native land. Therefore, while we rejoice when we hear of successful achievement on the part of our brethren in other lands, we can only heave a deep sympathetic sigh when we hear of their reverses and console ourselves with the knowledge that as in our good· so in our evil fortunes God is still with us, though in the latter instance it be with a chastening hand. It is this, I take it, that King Solomon meant when he said—"If thou seest the oppression of the poor and violent perversion of judgment in a province, marvel not at the matter; for He that is higher than the highest regardeth. So there be then higher than they."

They may, with no little advantage to themselves, regard this little volume who are foremost and loudest in racial denunciation.

A word regarding its scriptural allowability.

That it is forbidden to number Israel is generally conceded—especially after a calamitous visitation, either by epidemic or war—as deduced from King David's confession to its guiltiness to the prophet Gad, after a battle with his arch-enemy the Philistines,

INTRODUCTION.

when he took the strength of his surviving army; for the strength of Israel lies not in their number but in their Protector, and in no instance do we find an entire census of them taken, excepting in the introduction of Jacob and his family into Egypt, for the purpose of future comparison. In accordance then with this precedent it has not been the intention to give a census of the Jews of the United Kingdom but a business reference of "Rosh B'nai Israel," the heads of the families established in mercantile pursuit in this country.

It is recorded, somewhere, that the ancient Britons were among the Roman detachment at the siege of Jerusalem, and that they were the most zealous in the application of the torch to the temple. Many a century has since revolved round the wheel of time, and though they have themselves become extinct as a people, their successors of to-day—they cannot be termed survivors—do harbor a large portion of their number and are on most amicable terms with them, whilst the latter are a credit both socially and financially to the country that was among the first to oppress them and the first to plant the standard of civil and religious tolerance. Who knows—for who can be so blind as not to see the practical Finger of Providence in all this—but that this country, one of the instruments of chastisement, may yet prove to become the first to say unto them, "Our hearts will go with you to your own native land,

INTRODUCTION.

for we have heard that God is with you."—And in that day shall Israel be the third with Egypt and with Assyria, a blessing in the midst of the land: whom the Lord of Hosts shall bless, saying, Blessed be Egypt my people, and Assyria the work of mine hands, and Israel my inheritance." She who, like those countries, was among the first to oppress, may become God's first honored instrument in reclaiming that bit of land for them adjacent its African occupancy, and, in union with the sheltering wing of our Royal Father, constitute herself its protectorate. Then, indeed, will the words be realised which He spoke by Isaiah, in this latter time, as it was in the days of the Babylonian return, as expressed by Nehemiah—"And it shall come to pass in that day, that the remnant of Israel, and such as are escaped of the house of Jacob, shall no more stay upon him that smote them; but shall, in truth, stay upon the Lord, the Holy One of Israel. The remnant shall return, even the remnant of Jacob, unto the mighty God."

London, July 6, 1893—5653.

THE EDITOR.

N.B.—Owing to some unforseen circumstances, coupled with the rather too protracted delay of its publication, we regret that this is not in as complete a form as we could wish, and promise in the second a more amplified edition.

THE PUBLISHERS.

ENGLAND.

BATH

Commercial Directory of the Jews of Gt. Britain.

Aarons, Mrs. ; Fancy goods.
Franks, M. ; Financier.
Goldsmith ; Boot and shoe manufacturer.
Green ; Outfitter.
Leon ; " Pluto Steel Works," Sheffield.
Sloman ; Dye works.
Somers, R., 7, Railway Place ; Master tailor and outfitter.

BIRKENHEAD, CHESHIRE.

Bernstein, Jacob, 42, Argyle Street ; House-furnisher.
Black, E., 334, Price Street ; House-furnisher and general draper.
Bloom, Arnold, 52, Argyle Street ; House-furnisher and general draper.
Gorfunkle, E., 91, Price Street ; Complete house-furnisher.
Hillenberg, Moses, 111 ; Jeweller.
Himes, W. H., 8, Grange Road, W. ; Dealer in pianos and music.
Morris, A., 143, Conway Street ; Complete house-furnisher, draper, clothier, etc.

BLACKBURN, PRESTON.

Commercial Directory of the Jews of Gt. Britain.

BLACKBURN.

Ardleigh Range.
Pinkus, A. ; Draper and general dealer.

Bolton Street.
Weller, J., 51 ; Picture frame maker.

Feilden Street.
Aaron, I., 53 ; Picture and general dealer.

James Street.
Goldman ; Financial agent.

Mincing Lane.
Saks, Samuel, & Co. ; Chamois leather manufacturer and sponge merchant. Est. 1882.

Northgate Street.
Rosenson, 45 ; Glass dealer and contractor.

Regent Street.
Kujawski, Jos., 46 ; Waterproof garment manufacturer; also practical chiropodist. Est. 1876.

PRESTON.

Avenham Lane.
Aaron Bros. ; Complete house furnishers. Branch, 4, Francis Passage, Lancaster.

BLACKBURN.

Commercial Directory of the Jews of Gt. Britain.

Friargate.

Klein, Joseph, 126 ; Cycle agent and house furnisher. Est. 1883.

Lancaster Road.

Goodman, M., 47 ; Glass and plumbers' supply.

Walker Street.

Goodman, S., 43 ; Chamois leather dresser.

BOSTON, LINCOLN.

Cheapside.

Glass, Saml., 23 ; Cabinet and picture frame-maker

Dolphin Lane.

Lipman, A., 23 ; Wholesale and retail cigarette maker and tobaconist.

High Street.

Robinson, Wolf, 42 ; Wholesale and retail picture frame maker, gilder, and importer of mouldings.

Market Place.

Szapira, A., Mrs., 39 ; Jeweller and antiquarian.
Szapira, S., 39 ; Jeweller and antiquarian.
Wolman, S. (Rev.), 39 ; Reader Hebrew Cong.

Maud Foster Terrace.

Rubinstein, S., 7 ; Cabinet maker.

BOSTON.

Commercial Directory of the Jews of Gt. Britain.

SHIRBECK.
Leo, A., Miss ; Leo House.

SPAIN LANE.
Harris, Lewis, 9 ; Master tailor.

STATION STREET.
Szapira, M., 20 ; Wholesale and retail jeweller, etc.

WIDE BARGATE.
Canin, Bros., 37 ; Wholesale and retail fine art dealers, picture-frame makers, and importers of mouldings.

WORMGATE.
Padwell, S., 9 ; Tully's Court ; Cabinet maker.

LINCOLN.
Birmbaum, J. ; Financial agent.
Lichtenheim, M. ; Furnisher.
Lyons ; Financial agent.

BRADFORD, YORKS.

BANK STREET.
Rosenthal, I, 32 ; Havana cigar importer.

BRADFORD.

Commercial Directory of the Jews of Gt. Britain.

Bridge Street.
Furstenheim, M ; Stuffs and woollens.

Chapel Street.
Levy, A., & Co., 1–3 ; Stuffs and woollens.
Zossenheim & Partners, 30 ; Stuffs.

Grove Terrace.
Loewy, Julius Isaac, 35 ; Inquiry and debt collecting office of the British and Foreign Equitable Trade Association. And at Southport.

Hall Ings.
Bernstein, W. F., 27 ; Stuffs and woollens.
Landa and Bernstein, 2 ; Tailors' trimmings and woollen rag merchants.

James Street.
Feinburgh, Wm., 16–11, Godwin Street ; Tailor and outfitter.

John Street.
Mendlesohn, S., 14 ; Practical tailor and cutter.

Leeds Road.
Gottheil & Sons, 35 ; Woolen merchants.

Little Horton Lane.
Wolfe, Abm., 5 ; Bradford Union Advance Bank.

BRADFORD, YORKS.

Commercial Directory of the Jews of Gt. Britain.

MANCHESTER ROAD.

Bernstein. Abm., 29; Jewelry and musical instruments.

Bernstein, Benj., 27; Clothier, outfitter, and manufacturer of ladies' mantles and costumes.

Rosenberg, Percy M., & Co., 17, 18, 12; Watches, clocks, jewelry, and general merchants.

Shrenski, M., 9, Lumby Street; Wholesale clothier.

MANNINGHAM LANE.

Maizels, A., 35, Lupton Street; Wholesale and retail jeweller and clothier.

Marks, D., 42, Victoria Street; Waterproof manfr.

Robinson, Hy., 31, Hanover Square; Wholesale and retail jeweller and draper.

NORTHGATE.

Morris, J., 56; Practical tailor and cutter.

Sunderland, I., 52; Military and naval tailor.

PECKOVER STREET.

Meyer, A., & Co., 27; Merchants.

THORNTON ROAD.

Aaronson, G., 15; Bill discounter.

TYRRELL STREET.

Leon, Sydney; Yorkshire and Lancaster Advance Bank.

VICAR LANE.

Edelstein, Moser, & Co.; Merchants.

BIRMINGHAM.

Commercial Directory of the Jews of Gt. Britain.

Aston.

Jacobs, Jacob, St. Helens's House. Birmingham and Aston Loan Society.

Aston Road.

Harris, Lewis, Forester House, 64. Merchant tailor.

Marks, I., Aston Brook House. Merchant tailor.

Aston Street.

Cohen, David, 83. Clothier and outfitter.

Balsall Heath Road.

Cohen, Chas., 121. Tailor and draper.

Belgrave.

Grosbaum & Sons. China merchants.

Bishops Street.

Abrahams, Reuben, 200. Master tailor.

Brown, John, 36. Master tailor.

Coleman, S. & J., 51. Master and custom tailor.

Bordesley.

Shrank, H., 161, High Street. Complete house and office furnisher.

BIRMINGHAM.

Commercial Directory of the Jews of Gt. Britain.

BROMSGROVE STREET.

Brown, Jacob, 113. Master tailor.

Kalisher, P., 38. Rag merchant and tailors' trimmings.

BULL STREET.

Lewis's Merchants.

Harris, J. & Sons. Dyers.

Samuel, B., 60. Pawnbroker and jeweler.

COLMORE ROW.

Aaron, J., 15. Silversmith, jeweler, and gun merchant.

COMMERCIAL STREET.

Hyman, Henry, 10. Custom and master tailor.

Silverstone, Meyer, 9. Master tailor.

CONSTITUTION HILL.

Davis, Isaac, 87. High-class tailor and outfitter.

Goldman, Hyman, 39. "The Forward Clothing Establishment."

Levi, P. F., 5 and 6. Merchant tailor and clothier.

CORPORATION STREET.

Davids, D., 26. Solicitor.

BIRMINGHAM.

Commercial Directory of the Jews of Gt. Britain.

CREGOE STREET.

Nathan, Jos., 66. Master trouser manufacturer.

Singer, Harris, 59. Master tailor.

DALE END.

Belman, N., 51. Jeweller and pawnbroker.

Newman, Benj., 67 and 68. Furniture dealer.

DEAN STREET.

Moses, Jac. (Jac. Simons, foreman), 4. Master tailor.

DERITEND.

Greenberg, M., 213, High Street. High-class tailoring establishment.

Veiner, M., 45, Penn street, and 67-69, Heathmill lane, and at 104, Lister street. Pawnbroker and clothier.

DIGBETH.

Goldman, Jos., 70. Practical tailor and general outfitter.

DUDLEY STREET.

Rosenberg and Neufliess. Clothing manufacturers.

EDGBASTON STREET.

Abrahams, A., 29. Pipe manufacturer.

BIRMINGHAM.

Commercial Directory of the Jews of Gt. Britain.

Frederick Street.

Blanckensee J. and Co., 48(w)   Watch manufacturers.
Cohen, A., and Son, 27.   Diamond merchants.
Cohen, A. D., 43(w),   American merchants.
Danziger and Isaacs, 41(a), Bread manufacturers.
David, H., 31.   Diamond Merchant.
Davis, M., 21.   Gold chain maker.
Levi, S. M., 16.   Gilt jewelry manufacturer.
Lyon, S., 301.   Jeweler.
Summer, J., 22.   Jeweler's factor.
Warschauer, S., 26.   Export merchant.

Gooch Street.

Caro, Robert, 246.   Bootmaker.
Cohen, Jac., 38.   Master tailor.
Harris, J., 52.   High-class tailor and outfitter.
Marks, Henry, 148.   Merchant tailor and outfitter.

Gough Street.

Dresden, Meyer, 29 (upper).   Master tailor.
Isaacs, Harris, 21.   Master tailor.

Great Colmore Street.

Barnett, Michael, 6.   Fashionable custom tailor.

BIRMINGHAM.

Commercial Directory of the Jews of Gt. Britain.

Great Hampton Row.

Richardson, Hyman, 93. Tailor and woollen draper. Est. 1866.

Great Hampton Street.

Davis, Bernhard, 58. Merchant tailor and outfitter.

Peters, D., 3. Tailor and outfitter.

Hill Street.

Dight, M. L., and Sons, 7. Wholesale opticians.

Hockley Hill.

Braham, E. F., 53. Wholesale jeweler.

King & Son, 108. High-class tailors and mantle-makers.

Lotheim, M. & S., (st). 6. Wholesale jewelers.

Sachs. & Co., 20 (st). Wholesale jewelers.

Scott, A., 62. Manufacturing jeweler, clock and watch importer, and general factor.

Holloway Head.

Abrahams, Jos,, 17, Blucher street. Tailor.

Berkowitz, Harris, 10, Florence street. Tailor.

Cohen, Hyman, 63. Wholesale and retail slipper manufacturer.

Gold, Jacob, 19, Florence street. Master tailor.

BIRMINGHAM.

Commercial Directory of the Jews of Gt. Britain.

Jacobs, Morris, 19, Ellis street. Wholesale slipper manufacturer.

Joseph, S., & Co., Wholesale cabinet manufacturers.

Levi, B., Mrs., 82. Pawnbroker and jeweler.

Levy, Mark, 116. Dealer in watch materials.

Loffman, Jac., 72. Tailor.

Melcher, S., 50. Grocer and provision dealer.

Shmaman, S.. 1, Florence street. Glass dealer.

Stock, Em., 10, Sutton street. Master tailor.

Horse Fair.

Abrahams, Raphael, 141, Irving street. Tailor.

Glass, L., 133, Irving street. Tailor.

Hollander, Jeweler.

Jacobs, Ph., 152, Irving street. Tailor.

Hurst Street.

Bernstein, Jac., 19, Inge street. Tailor.

Engleman, Jac., 39, (lower). Clothier.

Goldstein, A., 20, Inge street. Tailor.

Hassel, Lewis, 39, Thorp street. Tailor.

Isaacs, Sol., 47, Thorp street. Tailor.

Lester, Em., 38, Thorp street. Tailor.

BIRMINGHAM.

Commercial Directory of the Jews of Gt. Britain.

Levy, Sam 43, Inge street. Boot and shoe finisher.
Solomon, Simon, 45, Inge street. Tailor.
Yellowitz, Isaac, 14, Court Inge street. Tailor.

ICKNIELD STREET.

Levy, E., 265. Manufacturer of gilt watch-keys swivel-keys, brooch-tongs, etc.

JAMAICA ROW.

Davis, D.H., 87. Fashionable tailor and outfitter.

KENT STREET.

Savitz, Sol., 72. Master and custom tailor.

LANCASTER STREET.

Horowitch, Freda, Mrs., 108. Pawnbroker.

LATIMER STREET, SOUTH.

Cash, Israel, 59. Master tailor.

LIVERY STREET.

Davis, D. and M., 2 and 3. Antique dealers and silversmiths.

LOWER ESSEX STREET.

Cave, J., 29. Master tailor.
Cohen, Marks, 78. Master tailor.

BIRMINGHAM.

Commercial Directory of the Jews of Gt. Britain.

Lower Tower Street.
Cassell, Abm., 71. Pawnbroker and jeweller.

McDonald Street.
Hoff, R., 12. Master tailor.

New Street.
Phillips, 49. Furrier.

Newhall Street.
Levi and Salamon, 143. Wholesale Jewellers.

New Town Row.
Rosenthal, Morris, 49. Practical tailor and draper.
Rubenstein, B., 92. Wholesale jeweler, watch-maker, and pawnbroker.
Solomon, Isaac, 31. Clothier and outfitter.

Oozells Street.
Blaiberg and Marson, Bute Works. Engineers.

Parade.
Cohen, Jac., 79. Merchant-tailor and outfitter.
Goldberg, I. A., 46. Fancy draper and hosier.
Goldman, Henry, 56. Practical tailor and outfitter.
Levi, Hyman, 130, Sandpits. Wholesale and retail tailoring, and tailors' trimmings.

BIRMINGHAM.

Commercial Directory of the Jews of Gt. Britain.

Levy, & Co., 146, Sandpits. Manufacturers of German-silver watches, watch-cases, and outside protecting cases, etc.

Pershore Street.

Seager, Harris, 57. Custom and master tailor.

Sherlock Street.

Lesser, Herman, 41. High-class tailor and outfitter.

Peters, Benj., 33. High-class tailor and outfitter.

Samuel, Lewin P., 30. Pawnbroker and jeweller.

Wolf, William, 126. Pawnbroker and jeweller.

Singer's Hill.

Emanuel, Rev. B. J., B.A., Minister.

Fink, Rev. J. Reader.

Wolf, Rev. Assistant reader and collector.

Smallbrook Street.

Emanuel Bros., 98. Pawnbrokers and jewellers.

Muslin, Barnett, 83. Merchant tailor.

Thomas, Isaac, 85. House and office furnisher.

Thomas, Myer, 24. House and office furnisher.

Wolfe, H., 18a. Wholesale boot and slipper manufacturer.

BIRMINGHAM.

Commercial Directory of the Jews of Gt. Britain.

SMITHFIELD STREET.

Simon, D. & Son, 26. and 65, Benacre street. Pawnbrokers and clothiers,

SNOW HILL.

Greenberg, S. H., 27. Civil and military tailor.

Isaacs & Co., 88, Shadwell street. Bedding and furniture manufacturers.

Levi, H., 68. "The Snow Hill Clothing Stores."

Lyons, M., 4. Wholesale jeweller and diamond merchant. Est. 1816.

STAFFORD STREET.

Cohen, Jos., 70-71, "Justice House." Tailor and outfitter.

Marks, E., 47-48. Tailor and outfitter.

Simons, S., 1. Tailor and clothier.

STATION STREET.

Cassell, Jac., 2-3. Furrier. Branches: Coventry, Leamington, Walsall, Wolverhampton, Dudley, and Leicester.

STRATFORD ROAD.

Woolf, G., 92. Pawnbroker and jeweler.

BIRMINGHAM.

Commercial Directory of the Jews of Gt. Britain.

Suffolk Street.

Brooks, Jos., Suffolk Buildings. Picture-frame manufacturer, etc.

Gordon, Warwickshire Furnishing Co.

Summer Hill Road.

Luntz, M., 74. Complete house-furnisher.

Summer Hill Terrace.

Brenholz, H. D., 29; Jeweler and diamond merchant.

Cotton, A. Jeweler.

Marcuson, D. I., Bros. & Asher. Jewelers' factors.

Summer Lane.

Balcon, L., & Co,, 116, "The Hall of Fashion." Tailors and outfitters.

Coleman, Henry, 162. Tailor and outfitter.

Peters, H., 20. Tailor and outfitter.

Vittoria Street.

Goldsmid, M. J., 67. Wholesale jeweler.

Jacobs, E. & Son, 88. Wholesale jewelers.

Levetus, Bros., 47. Jewelers.

Levetus, E., 47. Electro-plate manufacturer.

Spiers & Co., 45. Silversmiths.

BIRMINGHAM.

Commercial Directory of the Jews of Gt. Britain.

Vyse Street.

Abrahams, Bros., 72.   Wholesale jewelers.
Abrahams, S., 119.   Diamond broker.
Cohen, J., 2.   Precious stone dealer.
Greenberg & Co., 22.   Jewelers.
Harman & Co., 78.   Jewelers.
Isenberg, J., 46.   Watch manufacturer.
Landau, J.   Dealer in jewelers' requisites.
Nathan Bros., 120.   Ring makers.
Wolffe Bros., Watch manufacturers.

Warstone Lane.

Abrahams, L., 163, E.   Jewelers' factor.
Ahronsberg Bros., 27.   Wholesale jewelers.
Levy, D., 45.   Watch manufacturer.
Myers, J. & Sons, 189.   Wholesale jewelers.
Sumner, F., 167.   Seal engraver.

Wrentham Street.

Joseph, Alex., 20.   Master coat maker.
Singer, Sam., 26.   Master tailor.

Wrottesley Street.

Lintine & Co., Wholesale bicycle fittings and accessories makers.

1A

BRIGHTON.

Commercial Directory of the Jews of Gt. Britain.

ADELAIDE CRESCENT.

Cohen, Edgar, 10 ; Merchant.
Cohen, Misses A. L., 14 ; Private.
Davidson, L., 11 ; Merchant.
Goldsmid, Miss, Palmyra Square ; Private.
Henriques, A. G., J. P., 9 ; Retired.
Marks, I. M., 34 ; Stockbroker.
Sassoon, Mrs. F., 37 ; Private.
Wagg, Arthur ; Retired.
Worms, Baron de, 27 ; Retired.

BOND STREET.

Bennosan, M. ; China and glass merchant.
Costa, I. de ; Cigar merchant.

BRUNSWICK TERRACE.

Lewis, S., 13 ; Retired.

BUCKINGHAM PLACE.

Cohen, A., 49 ; Retired.
*Springer, W., 24 (road); Fancy goods and commission agent.

CHURCH STREET.

Lyons, L., 3 ; Clothier and outfitter.

COMPTON AVENUE.

Costa, Miss de, 41 ; Private.

DEVONSHIRE PLACE.

Goldberg, W. ; Retired

BRIGHTON.

Commercial Directory of the Jews of Gt. Britain.

Duke Street.

Moss, H., 5 and 21 ; Clothier and outfitter.
Shaffran, Isaac, 20 ; Hairdresser, perfumer, and wig-maker ; Teeth cleansing a specialty. Est. 1880.
Trennar, Mrs., 26 ; Ladies' wardrobes.

Easter Terrace.

Sassoon, Sir Albert, Bart., K.G.S.I.

Edward Street.

Davison, 85 ; Confectioner.

First Avenue.

Sassoon, Aaron T., 35 ; Merchant.

Gardner Street.

Baum, H. ; Cutlery and plated goods.
Jones, H., 7 ; Clothier and outfitter.

Grand Parade.

Lorie, S., 15 ; Retired.

Gloucester Street.

Cohen, J. ; Financial agent.

Hampton Place.

Myers, H. H. ; Solicitor.

King's Road.

Adelstone, J., 37 ; Jeweller and antique dealer.
Andrad, S. H. ; Stockbroker.
Barron, J., 34 ; Dealer in works of art.
Bevan, J., 11 ; Dealer in works of art.

BRIGHTON.

Commercial Directory of the Jews of Gt. Britain.

Cohen, M., 80 ; Dealer in engravings, etc.
Davis, J. L., 51 ; Financier and dealer in works of art.
Koppenhagen ; Dealer in fancy goods.
Lewis, N. & Son, 44 : Jewellers and dealers in works of art to H.M. the Queen.
Marx, C., 1, East Street ; Jewelry and diamonds.
Marx, Mrs. W., 66 ; Jeweller and silversmith.
Sassoon, Arthur ; Merchant.

LANDSDOWN STREET.

Cohen, Mrs. M., 9 ; Private.

LITTLE RUSSELL STREET.

Davis, B. F. ; Dealer in fancy goods.

LONDON ROAD.

Cohen, J., 9; and 31, Gloucester Street; City discount and bank financial agent.
Reichman, S., 60 ; House furnisher.

MEETINGHOUSE LANE.

Jones, L., 18 ; General dealer.
Kulp, M., & Son, 24 ; House furnishers.

MONTPELIER ROAD.

Harris, Mrs. L. ; Private.
Jewell, Mrs. S. ; Private.

NORTH ROAD.

Cohen, S. H., 2, Tichbourne Street ; Matter tailor.
Jacobson, M., 9 ; Retired.

BRIGHTON.

Commercial Directory of the Jews of Gt. Britain.

NORTH STREET.
Davis, W., & Sons, 27 and 58 ; Jewellers, etc.

ORIENTAL PLACE.
Harris, J., 35 ; African merchant.
Mendelson, Mrs. ; Private.

OVER STREET.
Morris, E., 15 ; Traveller.

PELHAM SQUARE.
Costa, Alf de ; Bookmaker.

PRESTON PARK AVENUE.
Hart, R., 18 ; Retired.

PRESTON ROAD.
Cook, S., "Montrose" ; Retired.
Harfield, Miss J. M. ; Private.
Phillips, S. M., 71 ; Retired.
Ulman, Jos., "Renby" ; Diamond merchant.

PRESTON STREET.
Mannie, J., 43 ; Dealer in works of art.
Newton, Mrs., 33 ; Private.

QUEEN'S GARDENS.
Sassoon, Reuben D. ; Merchant.

QUEEN'S PARK ROAD.
Crook, Wolf, 131 ; Master tailor.

QUEEN'S ROAD.
Joel, M., 3 ; Tobacconist.
parker, I. S., Quadrant : Licensed victualer.

BRIGHTON.

Commercial Directory of the Jews of Gt. Britain.

Regent Square.
Keesing, Thos. H. ; Retired.

St. James Street.
Einstein, Mrs. ; Tobacconist.

Hyman & Son, 1 ; and at 3, Ship Street ; Hairdressers, wigmakers and hair specialists. Manufacturing perfumers to H.I.M. the Shah of Persia. Established 1881.

Shavenski, Rev. ; Reader Hebrew congregation.

Ship Street.
Phillips, H. W. ; Financial Agent.

Sudeley Terrace.
Ezra, 19 ; Steward to Sir Albert Sassoon.
Samuel, M., 11 ; Retired.

Sussex Street.
Hamilton, Dr. Lawrence, 30 ; Retired.

Synagogue House.
Jacobs, Rev. A. E. ; Min. and sec. Hebrew congregation.

Trafalgar Street.
Jones Julius, 79 ; Clothier and jeweller. Est. 1848.

Third Avenue.
Sassoon, Ed. E., 3 ; Merchant.

Wellington Road
Ulman, S,, 10 ; Diamond merchant.

BRIGHTON.

Commercial Directory of the Jews of Gt. Britain.

West Street.
Newman, A. ; Dealer in works of art.

Westbourne Terrace.
Levy, Mrs. E. ; Private.

Western Road.
Braham, Mrs., 38 ; Jeweller.
Harris, M. ; Dentist.

Windsor Street.
Hart, A., 6 ; General dealer.

York Street.
Cohen, Misses, 34 ; Private.

Board and Lodgings.
Lion, M. A., 8, Cavendish Place.
Natalie, Miss, 5, Waterloo Street.
Sultan, Mrs., Bedford Square.

WEST BRIGHTON.

HOVE.

Church Road.
Marks, B., 113 ; Pawnbroker, clothier and jeweller.

St. John's Terrace.
Jacobs, L., 32, Albany Villas ; Colonial merchant.
Marks, B. W. ; Colonial merchant.

BRIGHTON.

Commercial Directory of the Jews of Gt. Britain.

TISBURY ROAD.
Artom, Mrs.; Private.
Isaacs, 35; Financial agent.
Stern, G., 68; Retired.

COLLEGIATE.
The Drive.
Jewish Boarding School for Ladies, "Clopthorne," Mdme. Lewy, B.A., Principal; J. Lewy, Professor of French.

"POMBAL HOUSE."
Jewish Boarding School for Ladies, the Misses Pyke and Solomon Principals.

BRISTOL.

BARTON.
Morse, G. A., 15, St. James'; Cap manufacturer.
Simmons, Henry, 12, St. James'; Cap manufacturer.

BATH STREET.
Blankensee, M., & Son; Wholesale jewellers and general merchants.

BRIDGE STREET.
Lazarus, A.; Financier.
Salanson; Optician.

BROAD STREET.
Blankensee, F., & L.; Cider merchants.
Epstein, Joseph, 33; Wholesale picture frame manufacturer for home and export.

BRISTOL.
Commercial Directory of the Jews of Gt. Britain.

CASTLE STREET.
Weinberg, J., 62 ; Clothier and outfitter.

CLIFTON.
Michael, M., 45, Fernbank Road ; (Retired).
Pollack, J. (Rev.) ; Prin. Heb. Dept. Clifton College.

COTHAM.
Nathan, M. ; (Retired).

LODGE STREET.
Feigenbone, Archer, 4 ; Master tailor.

LONDON ROAD.
Schwarz, M., & J. ; General dealers.

NEWFOUNDLAND STREET.
Feather, H., 5, Barrs Street ; Tailor and outfitter.
Goldman, W., 12 ; Glass merchant and Stained glass contractor.
Millet Bros. ; Wholesale and retail drapers and haberdashers.

NICHOLAS STREET.
Could, A. ; Financier.
Zachari, M. ; Financier.

NORTH STREET.
Lyons, Misses ; Feather Cleaners.

PARADE.
Jessel, John, St. Augustine ; Pawnbroker, jeweller, and clothier.

BRISTOL.

Commercial Directory of the Jews of Gt. Britain.

Park Row.

Belcher, C. H., (Lower); Jeweller and general dealer.
Eisenberg, A. H. (Rev.); Reader Heb. Cong.
Moore, M.; (Retired).

Philadelphia Street.

Goldstone; Master tailor.

Redcliffe Hill.

Festenstein, F. & H.; Somerset Furnishing Company. wholesale and retail furniture manufacturers.
Israel, A., 50; Complete house-furnisher.
Lazarus, B. & S.; Pawnbrokers and jewellers.
Rosenthal, A., 38; Picture-frame manufacturer.

Russell Town.

Abelson, A., 4, Victoria Buildings; Pawnbroker, jeweller and clothier.

St. George's Road.

Wolfson, P., Woodwell Crescent; Picture-frames.

St. James' Square.

Cohen, A., 16; Master tailor.

St. Luke's Road.

Rosenberg, P., 5; Draper and general dealer.

St. Paul's Street.

Goldberg, H. & Son; Wholesale slipper manufacturer.
Jacobs & Co., 20; Wholesale boot and shoe merchants.

BRISTOL.

Commercial Directory of the Jews of Gt. Britain.

Shannon Court.
Mosely, Gerald ; Solicitor and Vice-Consul for U.S. to Bristol and districts.

Stapleton Road
Smollan, S. ; Pawnbroker, jeweller, and clothier.

Temple.
Rosenberg, B., 5, Victoria Square ; Draper.

Totterdown.
Joseph, N., 36, Windsor ; Tinware manufacturer.

Victoria Street.
Platnauer Bros., 10 ; Wholesale jewellers and manufacturers and importers of watches and clocks. Branches : Birmingham and Paris.

Wine Street.
Michael, W. & A. ; Wholesale and retail jewellers.

BURTON-ON-TRENT.

Derby Street.
Barnett, Henry, 40 ; Complete house-furnisher.

Moor Street.
Beirnstein, B., 95 ; Accountant and furniture dealer.

New Street.
Rich, Adolph, 122 ; Picture-frame manufacturer, glass merchant and importer of mouldings.

West Street.
Bloomberg, Alfred, 35 ; High-class tailor.

CHATHAM, KENT.

Commercial Directory of the Jews of Gt. Britain.

BANKS, ROCHESTER.

Lyon, John ; Upholsterer.
Salomons, B. J., (Rev.) ; Min. Mem. Syn.

LUTON ROAD.

Berliner, I. ; Broker.
Goodman, B. ; Broker.

HIGH STREET.

Barnett, B., 162 ; Clothier.
Harrison, Chas., 165 ; Butcher for congregation.
Samuel, Jos., 184 ; Wholesale and retail clothier.

RAILWAY STREET.

Hyman, Ph., 20 ; Financier.

RICHARD STREET.

Posner, Hy., 20 ; Master tailor.

WATT'S PLACE.

Franklin, D. M., 10 ; Picture-frame maker.
Woolf, Rachel, 4 ; Greengrocer and umbrella maker.

CHELTENHAM.

Goldberg, S. ; Pawnbroker and jeweller.
Hart ; Fleece Hotel.
Isaachor, Wolfe ; Optician.
Nestor, M. ; Cheltenham College.
Schnurman (Rev.) ; Min. Heb. Cong.
Sternberg, Mrs. ; Pawnbroker and jeweller.

COVENTRY.

Commercial Directory of the Jews of Gt. Britain.

BARRAS LANE.
Baum, M. ; Watch manufacturer.

CHAPEL FIELDS.
Cohen, P. ; Watch manufacturer.

FLEET STREET.
Margolies, S. ; Complete house-furnisher.

HOLYHEAD ROAD.
Friedlander, A. E. ; Watch manufacturer.

SPON STREET.
Silverston, F. ; (Retired.)

THE BUTTS.
Radges, M. & J., Argyle House ; Watch manfrs.

UNION STREET.
Auerhahn ; Foreign correspondent.
Kalker, E. ; Foreign correspondent.

WARWICK ROAD.
Harris, L. ; Manager for Cohen's Watch Factory.

DERBY.

LONDON ROAD.
Fineberg, Mark, 31 ; Wholesale and retail furnisher.

OSMASTON ROAD.
Brown, J. ; House-furnisher.

DOVER.
Commercial Directory of the Jews of Gt. Britain.

Bridge Street.
Spero ; American Dentist.

Liverpool Street.
Barnstein, Rev., J. ; Reader Hebrew congregation.

Market Square.
Hart & Co., Waterloo House ; Pawnbrokers, clothiers and jewellers.

Snargate Street.
Cohen, R. ; Jeweller and Silversmith.
Davis, I. J., 13 ; Furnisher and Silversmith.
Davis, John ; House-furnisher.
Davison, I., ; Dealer in Antiques and curiosities.
Lewis, L. ; Complete house-furnisher.
Lichtenberg ; Clothier and outfitter.

Collegiate.
Folkstone Road.
Minerva College ; The Misses Hart, Principals.

GATESHEAD, DURHAM.
Askew Road.
Isaac, Morris, 100 ; Pawnbroker, clothier, and general dealer.
Rothfield & Co., 118 ; and at 2, George Street ; Wholesale and retail picture-frame makers, and watchmakers and jewellers.

George Street.
Glickman, L., 14 ; General draper.

GATESHEAD.

Commercial Directory of the Jews of Gt. Britain.

MARIAN STREET.
Abrahams, Marcus, 62 ; Picture-frame manufacturer.

REDHEUGH BRIDGE ROAD
Bernstone, Zelig, 12–14 ; Gilder, and wholesale retail picture-frame manufacturer. Also draper.

REDHEUGH ROAD.
Adler, Eliezar, 128 ; Watchmaker and jeweller.

WARWICK STREET.
Wilkes, Sol., 6 ; Pawnbroker and clother.

GRIMSBY, LINCOLN.

ALBERT STREET.
Bloom, S. 103 ; Wall paper and pictures.
Zuesman, H. J., 143 ; Master tailor.

CLEETHORPE ROAD.
Abrahams, Moses, 86 ; Pawnbroker, jeweller, and clothier. Established in 1872.
Altman, C., 218 ; Watchmaker and jeweller.
Bernstein, S. J., 155 ; High-class bespoke tailor.
Cohen, B., 191 ; Merchant tailor. Est. 1869.
Goldman, S., 185 ; Watchmaker and jeweller.
Hitner, Jos., Austrian House ; General merchant.
Morris, L., 203 ; Practical tailor.
Ruben, Harris, 235–7 ; Clothier, jeweller, and general house-furnisher.
Starfield, Saml., 269 ; Watchmaker and jeweller.

GRIMSBY.

Commercial Directory of the Jews of Gt. Britain.

Wood, I., 11, Nacton Street ; Pawnbroker, tailor and clothier.

Freeman Street.

Grant, Abm., 63, Nelson Street ; Watchmaker.

Bennett, S., 20 ; and at 51, Kent Street; Wholesale glass merchant and importer, and picture frame manufacturer. Est. 1868 ; 10, Linen warehouse.

Harris, Henry, 32 ; Watchmaker, jeweller, and silversmith.

Isaac, M., 159 ; Practical tailor.

Kuntsmann, N., 144 ; Fashionable bespoke tailor.

Rosenberg, Harris, 102 ; Merchant tailor. Est. 1881.

Kent Street.

Moskow & Bloom, 71 ; Master tailors.

Orwell Street.

Green, M., 20 ; Financial Agent.

Oxford Street.

Bennett, Lewis, 59; and 2, Lord Street ; Wall paper merchant.

Reiter, L., 29 ; Draper and furniture dealer.

Victoria Street.

Jacobs, A., 57 ; Master tailor and tailor for the trade, and woollen merchant.

Taylor, Harris & Co., 67a, Victor Street, Tailors and outfitters.

HANLEY, STAFF.

Commercial Directory of the Jews of Gt. Britain.

GLADSTONE STREET.
Cohen, Saml., 15; Tailor and draper.
Finn, 1, 14; Draper.

HAVELOCK PLACE, SHELTON.
Price, Maurice, 2a; Merchant tailor and draper.

HIGH STREET.
Lewis, L., 25; Butcher.
Myers, Julian, 59, 76, 80; Boot and shoe dealer.

HOWARD PLACE.
Epstein, Morris, 5; Financial agent.

HOPE STREET.
Alexander, Jos., 89; Painter and glass dealer.
Jacobs, Kewell, 114; Paper and glass dealer.

MARKET STREET.
Goldberg, L., 45; Financier.

PARLIAMENT ROW.
Greenberg, Saml., 47; Merchant tailor.
Levin, J.; Sponge merchant.
Rotenberg, Myer, 4; Waterproof garment manfr.

PICCADILLY.
Alexander, Adolph, Piccadilly Buildings; Merchant tailor. Est. 1872.
Bandell, J., 76; Wall paper merchant.
Gershon, Saml.; Warwickshire Furnishing Company.

HANLEY.

Commercial Directory of the Jews of Gt. Britain.

York Street.
Leventhal, M., 4 ; Restaurant.
Sumberg, S. (Rev.) ; Synagogue house.

Burslem.

Newcastle Street.
Jacobson, I. ; Glass and paint dealer.

Nile Street.
Goldman, M. ; Draper.

Waterloo Road.
Livingstone, Geo , 13 ; and 22, Hope Street ; Wholesale and retail wall paper and glass merchant.

Longton.

Caroline Street.
Cohen, I., 14 ; Bespoke tailor.

Commerce Street.
Fresner, H., 12 ; Custom tailor.

High Street.
Epstein, M., 26 ; House-furnisher.

Market Street.
Goldstone, S., 9 ; Merchant tailor.   Est. 1876.

Stafford Street.
Jacobson, S., 47 ; Wholesale and retail wall paper merchant.

HARTLEPOOL.
Commercial Directory of the Jews of Gt. Britain.

WEST HARTLEPOOL.
Lotinga, M., & Co. ; Steam and ship brokers.

ADELAIDE STREET.
Cassel & Son ; General dealers.

ALBERT STREET.
Prinsky, M., 8 ; Tobacconist and fancy goods dealer.

CHARLES STREET.
Broady, B., 13 ; Clothier and draper.
Mosesson, J., 9 ; House-furnisher.

CHURCH STREET.
Abrahams, G. L., & Sons, 25 ; Silversmiths and jewellers.
Broady, J. ; Pawnbroker and clothier.

JERSEY STREET.
Levinson & Landsberg, 28 ; Master tailors.

LYNN STREET.
Abrahams, Israel, Lambton House ; Bill discounter.
Prinsky, Elias, $26\frac{1}{2}$; Watchmaker and jeweller.

MUSGRAVE STREET.
Yoffe, Jos., 62, 64, & 55 ; Clothier and jeweller.

STOCKTON STREET.
Levy, Bros., Dalton House ; Clothiers and boot merchants.

EAST HARTLEPOOL.
Barnett, Alex., High Street and Middlegate Street ; Tobacconist, hairdresser, and general dealer.
Kaufman, Isaac, 38 & 40, Northgate Street ; Pawnbroker, jeweller, etc.

HULL.

Commercial Directory of the Jews of Gt. Britain.

ANLABY ROAD.

Cutner, A., 22, Ocean Place; Importer of Havana and domestic cigars.

Guttenberg, A.; House-furnisher.

ANNE SREET.

Phillips, P. S., 2; Pawnbroker and jeweller.

CARR LANE.

Barnett, B., 63; Goldsmith and diamond merchant.

Maizels, J., Henry's Arcade; Watchmaker, jeweller, and diamond setter.

CASTLE STREET.

Sadolfsky, Marks, 6; Clothier and outfitter and foreign money exchange.

COMMERCIAL ROAD.

Kersh, Isaac, 9; Tailor and tobacconist.

DRYPOOL.

Stone, M., & Son, 52, Gt. Union Street; Wholesale and retail clothiers.

GREAT PASSAGE STREET.

Freeman, L., 1; Baker and provision dealer.

Sultan, E., 24; Draper's job dealer.

GREAT THORNTON STREET.

Shalgoskie, I., 54; High-class tailor.

Simon, Morris, 28; Ladies' and gentlemen's tailor.

HULL.

Commercial Directory of the Jews of Gt. Britain.

Hedon Road.

Rosenston, H., 283; Merchant tailor.

Hessle Road.

Bloom, S., 55; House-furnisher and draper.
Bush, Jos., 125; Watchmaker, jeweller, and optician.
Feitelberg, E., & Co., 15-17; House furnishers, clothiers, and bankrupt stock buyers.
Gerhold, W., 53; Tobacconist and confectioner; also cabinet maker and furniture dealer.
Markson, Saml., 33; High-class tailor.
Shoolberg, Eda, & Son, 193; Pawnbrokers, etc.

Holderness Road.

Leiberman, S., 3, Alexander Buildings; Pawnbroker, jeweller, and outfitter.

Humber Street.

Haberland & Glassman, 25, 26; Wholesale grocers and shipstores dealers.

Lowgate.

Goldbard, H., 16; Tailor and draper.

Market Place.

Feldman, H., Woollen merchant.
Feldman, M., Musical instruments.
Wacholder, S., 29; Wholesale and retail jeweller and pawnbroker.

Myton Gate.

Heller Bros., 41, 41½, 42; Wholesale Manchester warehousemen; also at 4, Marsdon Square, Manchester.

HULL.

Commercial Directory of the Jews of Gt. Britain.

Magner Bros, 17 ; Importers and general wholesale dealers.
Moss, David, 68 ; Watchmaker and jeweller.

Myton Place.

Bass, M., 3, 4 ; Clothier and seaman's outfitter.

Nile Street.

Kersh, A., 15 ; Custom tailor.
Kersh, Nathan, 28 ; Custom tailor.

Osborne Street.

Harris, J., 20 ; Boot, shoe, and slipper manufacturer.
Honigbaum, M, 100 ; Wholesale and retail dealer in tailors' trimmings, drapery and smallware.
Jacobs, J., 113 ; Tailor and woollen merchant.
Levinson, L., 66 ; New and second-hand clothier.
Rosenston, A., 101 ; Merchant tailor and wholesale and retail tailors' trimmings.

Porter Street.

Barnett, E., Mrs., 86 ; and at 5, Henry's Arcade ; Wholesale and retail tobacconist.

Prospect Street.

Goltman, S., 21 ; Wholesale and retail tobacconist and jeweller.

Queen Street.

Shibko, Lewis, 1 ; Diamond merchant, goldsmith, and jeweller. Est. 1866.

HULL.

Commercial Directory of the Jews of Gt. Britain.

Salthouse Lane.
Levi, M., 9; Pawnbroker, clothier and jeweller.

Walker Street.
Goldstein, L., & Co., 61; Branch warehouse, 2, Anlaby Road; Wholesale cabinet makers, etc. London factory, 41, New Inn, Curtain Road, E.C.

Waltham Street.
Leshinsky, Marks, 10; High-class tailor and draper.

Waterloo Street.
Levinson, P., 17; Pawnbroker, clothier and jeweller.

JARROW, DURHAM.

Ellison Street.
Goldbezg, S., 51; Clothier and outfitter.

Grange Road.
Osterman, H., 26; Wholesale and retail picture-frame maker.

Market Square.
Weinberg, T.; also at 26, South Street; Complete house-furnisher.
Zallewsky, J., 3; Pawnbroker, clothiet, and jeweler.

Monkton Road.
Spiegle, A., 74; Wall-paper and glass dealer.

Ormond Street.
Ellisson, S., 24; Clothier and outfitter.

LEEDS.

Commercial Directory of the Jews of Gt. Britain.

Albion Street.

Forster, J. M.; Fashionable Tailor, and scientific cutter.

Goldstein & Davies, 117; Master Tailors.

Basinghall Street.

Cohen & Josephy; Woolen merchants.

Beeston Hill.

Lubelski, D., Beeston Road Clothing Works; Wholesale clothing manufacturer. Est. 1873.

Boar Lane.

Kino Bros.; Merchant Tailors.

Marcan, L., 20, Aire street; French consul.

Marcan, M., New Station street; Woolen merchant.

Sloman, J., 23, Royal Exchange; Teazle and cigar merchant.

Bridge Street.

Alexander, Joseph, 51; Greengrocer, fish dealer and Tobacconist.

Altshuler, S. H., 26; Wholesale and retail tobacconist and cigarette manufacturer.

Cohen, H., 11; and 51, Regent street; Family grocer and provision dealer.

Cohen, Louis, 57; Grocer, and wholesale and retail wine dealer. Special "Kosher" wines for passover. Country orders solicited, and will receive prompt attention. Also at 86, Regent street; Baker and grocer.

LEEDS.

Commercial Directory of the Jews of Gt. Britain.

David, Harris, 46; and at 103, Regent street; Family butcher and poulterer. Country orders attended to.

Fisher, Louis, 18; Family butcher and poulterer. Orders from summer resorts, promptly attended to.

Freedman, Israel, 15; Dealer in job fent, and all kinds of cloth. Est. 1878.

Freedman, M., 60; Family butcher and poulterer.

Goldberg, H., 25; Dealer in woolen remnants and job lots.

Harris, Hyman, 54; and at 30, Hope street : Family butcher and German wurst and sausage manufacturer and poulterer. Est. 1876.

Hyman, Morris, 36; Wholesale and retail dealer in tailors' trimmings, cloths, etc.

Hyman, Samuel, 39; Family grocer and provision dealer.

Israeli, Abm. M., 71 ; Brunswick loan office.

Kleinberg, Ephraim, 65; Family butcher and poulterer.

Morris, Israel, 66; Baker, grocer, and provision dealer.

Rooms, Jacob, 59; Wholesale and retail dealer in imported spirits and liqueurs.

Rosenbloom, Mrs. E., 13; Family grocer and provision dealer. Est. 1878.

Rosencrantz, J., 35; Tailor, and cigar and tobacco dealer.

LEEDS.

Commercial Directory of the Jews of Gt. Britain.

BRIGGATE.

Fox, J. Dealer in China-ware.

Friend & West, 66; Bespoke Tailors.

Harrison, D., Wood street; Wholesale and retail clothier.

Hyam & Co., ltd. Clothiers, etc.

Marks, Morris, & Co. Professional true-fitting tailors.

Wolf, H. Tobacconist.

Wolf, S., Harrison street, Lead dealers.

CAMP ROAD.

Blasebalk, M., 11, Brunswick terrace. Wholesale and retail jeweller. Est. 1856.

Blashkey, Morris, 8, Samuel street; Bespoke Tailor and draper.

Cainer, Simon, 30, St. Alban's street; Wholesale slipper and boot manufacturer.

Cohen, Chas. H., 46, Glover street; Master Tailor and draper.

Fineberg, S., Brunswick terrace; Master tailor.

Frieder, L. & Son, Grove House Lane; Boot and slipper manufacturers.

Goodman, Morris, 11, Rockingham street; Wholesale and retail grocer and provision dealer.

Hernberg, Hyman, 41, Rockingham street; Bespoke tailor and outfitter.

Joseph, Benj., 6, Brunswick terrace; Wholesale clothier.

Joseph, Davis, 6, Brunswick terrace. Wholesale clothier.

LEEDS.

Commercial Directory of the Jews of Gt. Britain.

Ludski, Mrs., 26. Boarding house.
Rosenbaum, Harris, 19, Rockingham street. Bespoke tailor.
Rosenbaum. Jac., 4, St. Alban's street. Tailor and outfitter.
Rosenberg, Lazarus, 36, Cobourg street. Family grocer and provision dealer, and jeweler.
Saipe, J. M., 82, Elmwood street; Bespoke tailor and outfitter.
Schultz, Wm., 25, Cobourg street; Draper, and dress and mantle maker, and ladies tailor. Est. 1881.
Simons, Morris, 11, Elmwood street; Workshop, Three Legs Yard, Lowerhead Row; Wholesale cloth manufacturer.
Sinofsky, Sol., 32, Cobourg street; Bespoke tailor.
Starfield, Herman, 20, St. George's terrace; Wholesale jeweler and watch manufacturer. Est. 1874.
Umanski, Moses, 13, Cross Belgrave street; Physician
Weinstein, Rev. S., Belgrave street; Reader Marion pole synagogue.

COOKRIDGE STREET.
Hirsch & Josephys; Woolen merchants.

GUILDFORD STREET.
Isaacs, D.; Jeweller.
Niman, Mark, 7; High-class Tailor, and wholesale and retail tailor's trimming merchant.

HOPE STREET.
Cohen, Rev. J., Reader, Polish Synagogue.
Frais, Jac., 28; Master tailor.

LEEDS.

Commercial Directory of the Jews of Gt. Britain.

Harris, Moses, 81; Boot, shoe, and slipper manufacturer.
Levinstein, Simon, 81; Joiner and cabinet maker.
Levy, Ph., 22, Master tailor, Melbourne street mills.
Moses, Henry, 24; Master tailor.
Oldman & Isaac, 28; Master tailors.
Pearlman, S., 32; Leather merchant and currier.
Rubenstein, M., 22; Wholesale cabinet manufacturer.
Rosenthal, H., 85-7; Leather merchant.
Saffer, Nathan, 24; Master tailor.
White Bros., 22; Master tailors.

HUNSLET.

Lightman, V., Globe Works; Cabinet maker.

KIRKGATE.

Brash, J., Wholesale and retail jeweler.
Cohen, M., Jeweler.
Levi, Isaac, 74; Piece-goods and fent dealer.

LADY LANE.

Altman, H., 32; Bespoke tailor.
Cohen, Saml., 31; Mechanic.
Fineberg, Morris, Old Workhouse yard; Master tailor.
Fox, Ph., 33-40; Picture dealer, frame maker, and house-furnisher.
Friedenson, J. W., 31; Hebrew and general printer.
Friend, Herman, Old Workhouse yard; Master tailor.
Geskofsky, A., 36; Surgical instrument maker, and cutler.

LEEDS.

Commercial Directory of the Jews of Gt. Britain.

Goldman, Elkan; Boot, shoe and slipper manf.

Goldman, Simon, Pollard's Yard, Millgarth street; Master tailor. Est. 1871.

Greenberg, E., 2, Quarry Hill; Draper.

Joseph, Simon, Bainbridge buildings, Millgarth st.; Master tailor.

Layman, Archer, Old Workhouse yard; Master tailor.

Leventhall, J., 2, Millgarth street; Provision importer and oil merchant.

Ludman, Harris, Bainbridge buildings, Millgarth street; Master tailor.

Saipe, Saml., 10; Wholesale and retail tailors' and dressmakers' trimmings.

Weiner, J., Pollard's yard, Millgarth street; Master tailor,

Wine, B., & Son, 30; Leather merchants.

Lowerhead Row.

Cohen, A., 14; Jeweler.

Gordon, Warwickshire Furnishing Co.

Wolf, A.; House-furnisher.

Wolf, H.; Clothier.

Macaulay Street.

Adelstone, D.; Slipper manufacturer.

Marsh Lane.

Berkovitch, B., 75a; Tailor and wholesale and retail clothier.

Bland, Morris, 31; Wholesale and retail tailor.

Galfskey, M., 67-9; also 59, Kirkgate. Baker, provision dealer, and confectioner.

LEEDS.

Commercial Directory of the Jews of Gt. Britain.

Goldman, S. (I. Priceman), 72 ; Wholesale and retail clothier.

Wine, Saml., 42 ; Wholesale and retail clothier and outfitter.

MEADOW LANE.

Cohen, Moss, 52 : Tailor and draper.

Lipman, M. L., 3 ; High-class tailor.

MEANWOOD ROAD.

Alexander, Louis, 3, Crimbles street ; Watchmaker and jeweler.

Cohen, Joe, 24, Crimbles street ; Tailor and draper and general dealer.

Levi, J., 42, Crimbles street ; Wholesale sponge and brush importer, and chamois leather dresser.

Wolfson, H., 163 ; Tailor and outfitter.

MELBOURNE STREET.

Levy, Archie, Low Fold Mills ; Master tailor.

Harrison, Marks, Low Fold Mills ; Master tailor.

Narunsky, Morris, Low Fold Mills ; Wholesale boot and shoe manufacturer.

Abrahams, I. & Co., 117, Templar street ; Passover cake manufacturer and Passover provisions. Country orders received.

Baim, Saml., 19, Templar street ; General grocer and biscuit manufacturer, and Passover provisions and *matzo* baker.

Landa, C. 5-7, Templar street : Wholesale and retail dealer in drapery, cloths, and fents.

Levi, I., 41, Luke street ; Bespoke tailor.

LEEDS.

Commercial Directory of the Jews of Gt. Britain.

Parisian Tailoring Co., 173; Merchant tailors and costume makers. Samples and particulars.

Raisman, M., aud Son, 62, Templar street; Wholesale and retail wine and spirit merchants.

NORTH STREET.

Aber, David, 38, Byron street; Wholesale boot, shoe and slipper manufacturer.

Abrahamson, M., 28, Byron street; Wholesale and retail tailors' trimmings.

Benjamin, H., 23, Trafalgar street, and 13, Nile st.; Wholesale boot, shoe and slipper manufacturer.

Berinstone, Harris, 25, Nile street; Wholesale and retail tailors' trimmings and woolens.

Bodlender, Abram, 2, Carlton terrace; wholesale clothing manufacturer.

Cohen, Benj., 13, Byron street; Master tailor.

Cohen, Max, 41, Byron street; Family grocer and provision dealer and tobacconist.

Cohen, Mrs. W., 30, Milliner, and English and and German draper.

Forleser, Rev. F. H. 3, Northfield villas; Reader, Gt. Synagogue, Belgrave street.

Frieze, Myer, 54, Byron street; Retail draper, and pinafore dealer.

Goldman, Hyman, 46, Byron street; Retail poulterer. Country orders attended to.

Grossman, F., 47, Byron street; Wholesale boot, shoe, and slipper manufacturer.

Harris, Jacob, 27, Trafalgar street; Jeweler and watch dealer.

LEEDS.

Commercial Directory of the Jews of Gt. Britain.

Hyman, A., 13, 14, Darley street; Wholesale and retail jeweler. Est. 1871.

Jacobs, A., 95; North of England furnishing Co.

Labovitch, J., 105, Templar street; Grocer and provision dealer.

Landey J., 19, Trafalgar street, and 18, Nile street; Wholesale boot and slipper manufacturer.

Levy, Reuben, 28, Trafalgar street; Tailor, woolen merchant, and general outfitter. Excelsior loan office.

Levy, Rev. S. J., 36, Albert grove; Reader New Briggate Synagogue.

Lewis, A., Lovell street; Boot, shoe, slipper, and ankle-strap manufacturer for home and export. Est. 1878.

Lewis, Isaac, 11, Nile, and 10, back Nile street; Wholesale and retail dealer in woolen goods and drapery.

Lewis, Jahob, 33, Concord street; Wholesale slipper manufacturer.

Lieberman, Julius, 43, Byron street; Family butcher Country orders attended to.

Miron, Simon, 44, Byron street; Family grocer.

Myers, Mrs. R., 72, Byron street; Dealer in English and German drapery and trimmings.

Newstead, J., 56, Stamford street; Beadle and collector, Gt. Synagogue, Belgrave street.

Rosenthal, B., 10, Byron street; Family grocer and provision dealer.

Wolfson, S., 15, Northfield terrace; Jeweler.

LEEDS.

Commercial Directory of the Jews of Gt. Britain.

Park Lane.

Blackston, Morris, & Sons, Park Lane Mills ; Hat and fancy cap manufacturers, and general merchants.

Camrass, S. & Son, New Park-st. Mill; Wholesale clothing manufacturers.

Myers, Jacob, New Park street Mill ; Wholesale hat and cap manufacturer.

Regent Street.

Agulsky, Harris, 99 ; Confectioner and greengrocer.

Benjamin, L., 15, Saint street. Boot, shoe, and slipper manufacturer.

Davison, Marks, 80. Family butcher and poulterer.

Glicksman Sam, 107. Family baker. Country orders attended to.

Gombenski, C., 62. Family grocer and baker.

Goldman, A., 32. Family grocer and provision dealer.

Listfield, Simon, 99½ ; Family grocer and provision dealer.

Manham, Mrs. A., 95. Wholesale tea and provision dealer. Est. 1878.

Marks, Harris, 70. Wholesale and retail tailor and trimmings dealer.

Olofski, Eli, 7, Busfield street. Wholesale and retail boot, shoe and slipper manufacturer.

Price, Joseph, 23. Draper, clothier, and waterproof garment dealer.

Scheinberg, Marks, 28. Tobacconist, earthenware and general dealer.

LEEDS.

Commercial Directory of the Jews of Gt. Britain.

Silman, Louis, 41. Family grocer and provision dealer.

Ziff, Louis, 42. Leather merchant and grindery dealer; and boot and shoe manufacturer.

Roundhay Road.

Rayman, Julius, 27a. Jeweler and watchmaker. Est. 1887.

Stone, J., 11, Louis street, Jeweler.

St. Peter's Street.

Fox, Louis, 109. Grocer and provision dealer, and Master tailor.

Goldberg, J. M., 41, Duke street. Broker and dealer in second-hand goods.

Taylor, Louis, 107. Wholesale Clothier, Tailor and outfitter.

Skinner Lane.

Abrahams, Rev. M., 19; Min. Gt. Syn., Belgrave street.

Lyons, Jac., 59; Pawnbroker and clothier.

Telephone Street.

Cohen, Wolf, Low Close Mills. Master tailor.

Trinity Street.

Isaacs, Henry, 32; Importer of watchmakers' tools and materials.

Vicar Lane.

Cohen, Sol., 26, Black Swan yard; Master tailor.

Goodman, Lewis, 26; Wholesale and retail tailors' trimmings.

LEEDS.

Commercial Directory of the Jews of Gt. Britain.

Shapiro, J. H., 26, Black Swan yard; Master tailor.

Velinski, Simon, 20; tailor and outfitter.

WADE LANE.

Livingstons, L., 66; Family butcher and sausage manufacturer.

WORTLEY LANE.

Zabludow, S. J., 54; and at 82, Burley road. Fashionable Tailor. Est. 1888.

YORK PLACE.

Ash, S. & L., 2; Woollen manfs., and merchants.

Myers Bros., 27; and Queen street; Wholesale hat and cap merchants.

Zossenheim & Partners; Woolen marchants.

LEICESTER.

Commercial Directory of the Jews of Gt. Britain.

Belgrave Gate.
Weinberg. S., 85, 17 ; Tailor and clothier. Est. 1869.

Berners Street.
Dainow, H. J. (Rev.) ; Reader, Hebrew Cong.

Bowling-Green Street.
Hart, S., 13 ; Financial agent.

Burton Street.
May, G., 8 ; Master tailor.

Campbell Street.
Jacobs, J. A., Campbell House ; Glass, china, and ironmongery stores.

Church Gate.
Green, Marks, 47 ; Manufacturer and dealer in clock and watchmakers' and jewellers' materials.

Thomas, S. 23 ; House-furnisher.

East Bond Street.
Lazarus, David, 3 ; Hosier and general dealer.

Erskine Street.
Doffman, J., 2, Spa House ; Master tailor.

Gallowtree Gate.
Alexander, Isaac, 9 ; Merchant tailor. Est. 1886.

Gladstone Street.
Cohen, Sol., 87 ; Master tailor.

Rosen, L., 69 ; Master tailor.

LEICESTER.

Commercial Directory of the Jews of Gt. Britain.

GRANBY STREET.
Felstein, H., with J. Weinberg; Tailor and collector.
Saltiel, Louis, 4, Dover Street; Master tailor.
Solomon, Morris, Black Horse Hotel; Master tailor.
Weinberg, Julius, Black Horse Hotel; Master tailor.

HALFORD STREET.
Samuel, Barnett, 29; Auctioneer and accountant.

HAYMARKET.
Wacks Bros.; Clothiers.

HIGH STREET.
Joseph, P., 40; House-furnisher.

HIGHCROSS STREET.
Bernberg, H., 164; Pawnbroker and clothier.
Kowalski, N. J., 10½; Carver, gilder, picture-frame maker, glass dealer, and moulding importer.

HUMBERSTONE ROAD.
Dove, Samuel, 36A; Standard Furnishing Co.

LONDON ROAD.
Joseph, Joseph, 158; Retired.

NORTH EVINGTON.
Berger, E., & Co., Market Place; Wholesale clothiers.

QUEEN STREET.
Marks, A. & L.; Fruit merchants.

LEICESTER.

Commercial Directory of the Jews of Gt. Britain.

St. Martin's
Jacobs, H., & Co., 5½ ; Cigar manufacturers.

Silver Street.
Rothschild, B. & J., 22 ; Cigar manufacturer. Est. 1877.

Wimbledon Street.
Hart & Levy ; Wholesale and export clothiers.
Hart, Ald., Mayor of Leicester.

LIVERPOOL.

Ainsworth Street.
Bernstein, Louis, 1, Brown Street ; Master tailor.
Singer, M., 1, Brown Street ; Master tailor.

Anson Street.
Balsam, Hymam, 10 ; Master tailor.
Fagin, Sol., 4 : Wholsale and retail draper and clothier.

Basnett Street.
Jong, Paul de, Bon Marchè.

Benson Street.
Aarons, J., 8 ; Private hotel.

Breck Road.
Berliner & Hyman, 282 ; Breck Road Clothing and Outfitting Co. and Hosiery Supply.
Silverman, B., 176 ; Furnisher and glass merchant.

LIVERPOOL.

Commercial Directory of the Jews of Gt. Britain.

BROWNLOW HILL.

Blumenthal, Natham, 93; and 141, Copperas Hill; Butoher, poulterer, and provision dealer.
Dorffman, M., 68 : Family grocer and provision dealer.
Finestone, A., 83 ; Draper and clothier.
Friedman, Ephraim, 30; Grocer and provision dealer.
Ginsburg, Natham, 108 ; Grocer and foreign provision dealer.
Mogdon, J., 33, Blake Street; Uniform and custom tailor.
Schlesinger, H.. 64 ; Family butcher.

BRUNSWICK ROAD.

Best, L., 72 ; Hairdresser and chiropodist.
Epstone, M., 12, Gerald Street ; Draper, clothier, and house furnisher.
Rapoport, Simon, 17 ; Draper and clothies.
Reuben, S., 25 ; Draper and house furnisher.

BRUNSWICK STREET.

Dreyfus Bros. & Co., Corn merchants, London and Paris.

BYROM STREET.

Duckett, F., 70 ; Wholesale and retail plate glass merchant and insurance agent.

CASTLE STREET, S.

Barnett & Co., 16 ; Bankers and bullion dealers.
Frenck, M. J. ; N. & S. Wales, Ltd. ; also Cazeneau Street.
Yates, 37 ; Banker and bullion dealer.
Yates, D. E., 26 ; Banker and bullion dealer.

LIVERPOOL.

Commercial Directory of the Jews of Gt. Britain.

CHATHAM STREET.

Cohen, Jos. H., 65 ; Master tailor for Henochsburg & Ellis.
Peer, Lewis, 13 ; Master tailor.

CLARENCE STREET.

Lyonson, A., 12 ; The Clarence Clothing, Drapery, and General Supply Co. ; clothing supplied on easy terms.
Myers, M., 10; Wholesale and retail cap manufacturer.
Nurick, H., 18 ; Wholesale and retail draper.

CLAYTON SQUARE.

Freeman, H., 7 ; Merchant tailor and draper.

COMMUTATION ROW.

Abrahams, H., 12 ; Tailor and outfitter.

CROWN STREET.

Black, Isaac, 11; Draper, clothier, and house-furnisher.
Coplan, M., 6, Sherdley Street ; Draper and general dealer.
Davis, Isaac, 17, Moon Street ; Wholesale stationer.
Goodman, Maurice, 61 ; Wholesale and retail draper and clothier.
Lazarus, S., 15, Moon St. ; Draper and general dealer.
Ledermann, L., & Sons, 19, Moon Street; Drapers and clothiers.
Mass, S., 27, Moon St. ; Draper and general dealer.

LIVERPOOL.

Commercial Directory of the Jews of Gt. Britain.

Myers, J., 73; Wholesale and retail Hebrew and English bookseller and binder.

Symon, Adolf, 34; Agent for Russian hemp.

Tavriger & Black, 7; Clothing manufacturers for home and export.

Weinstein, Nathan, 23, Moon Street; Wholesale and retail draper.

Wertheimer, M., 144; Coal merchant.

DAULBY STREET.

Norman, N., 21; Passenger agent.

DERBY ROAD, W.

Rabinowitz, Jac., 174; Draper, picture-frame maker, and glass merchant.

Stam, Louis, 98; Wholesale and retail window and looking-glass warehouse.

DERBY STREET, W.

Cowen, J. A., 53; Manchester and Glasgow warehouseman and wholesale clothing manufacturer.

Gilhooley, A., 20; Draper and furniture broker.

Serabski, Saml., 57; General warehouseman.

DUKE STREET.

Morris, J., 109; Passenger agent. American hotel. Established 1875.

Lewis, S., M.D., 155; Physician.

EDGEWARE STREET.

Harris, P., 9; Draper and general dealer.

LIVERPOOL.

Commercial Directory of the Jews of Gt. Britain.

Erskine Street, E.

Finger, Abm., 25 ; Wholesale jeweller and diamond merchant.

Everton Brow.

Bialy, D., 29A ; Wholesale cabinet maker.
Black, Daniel, 56 ; Draper, clothier, and house-furnisher.
Halpern, Simon, 82 ; General draper, clothier, and house furnisher.
Kaufman, B., 31–33 ; Manufacturer of dining and drawing-room suites and upholsterer.

Exchange.

Jackson ; Cotton merchant.
Rosenheim & Co. ; Cotton merchants.

Fairclough Lane.

Cohen, D., 6 ; and 83, Pembroke Place ; Grocer, provision dealer, and chandler.
Eddlestone, Ada, Miss, 26, Montague Street ; Grocer and provision dealer.

Fenwick Street.

Dreyfus, J., & Co. ; Corn merchants.
Meyer, A., & Co. ; Merchants.

Frederick Street.

Greenkraut, D., 11 ; Vest and trousers manufacturer.
Samuels & Bernstein, 17 ; Master tailors.

LIVERPOOL.

Commercial Directory of the Jews of Gt. Britain.

GILL STREET.

Barnett, Saul, 28 (back) ; Wholesale cabinet manfr.
Cohen, Abm., 21 ; Master tailor.
Stillman, A., 25 ; Master tailor.

GRANBY STREET.

Bernstine, M., 23 ; Wholesale jeweller.
Cohen, Bernard, 53 ; Wholesale and retail picture-frame manufacturer.

GT. GEORGE STREET.

Broude, Saml., 51 ; Furniture dealer and draper.
Harris, Wm., 40 ; Artistic decorator.
Harrison, I., 111 and 26 ; Complete house-furnisher and picture-frame manufacturer.

GT. HOMER STREET.

Cohen Bros., 89 ; and 24, Derby Road, Bootle, and Victoria Road, New Brighton ; Clothing stores.
Cohen, F., 229A ; Wholesale cabinet manufacturer.
Gorfunkle, L., 209 ; Complete house-furnisher.
Sandeman, A., 241 ; Draper and silk mercer.

GT. HOWARD STREET.

Gulnick, 316 ; Seaman's outfitter.
Hyams, Julius, 43 ; Jeweler and general outfitter.
Samuels, Morris, 134 ; Jeweller and outfitter.
Zembal, Ezekiel, 127 ; Watchmaker and outfitter.

LIVERPOOL.

Commercial Directory of the Jews of Gt. Britain.

GT. NEWTON STREET.

Bernstein, S., 47 ; Master tailor.
Davis, Jac., 22 ; Master tailor.

GT. ORFORD STREET.

Goldstone, M., 42 ; Master tailor for Lewis's.
Harris, I., 4 ; Master tailor.
Jacob, Simon, 32 ; Master tailor.
Katzin, J, 6 ; Bakery, 5, Pomona Street ; Wholesale and retail baker and general dealer.
Liverman, Ph., 39; Traveller for E. Black, Birkenhead.
Neuman, Moses, 18, Bittern Street ; Master tailor.
Pellish, H., 14 ; Wholesale and retail draper.
Syder, S., 39 ; Wholesale clothier.

GREGSON STREET.

Cantor, Harris, 140 ; Draper.
Harris, H., 117 ; Draper and general dealer.
Swede, R., 118 ; Draper and general dealer.

HALL LANE.

Myers, Morris, 40, Guelph Street ; Tailor and draper.

HANOVER STREET.

Frece, Isaac de, 97 ; Lyceum chambers ; Theatrical American lithographer.
Prag, George, 97 ; Lyceum chambers ; Wholesale jeweller.

LIVERPOOL.

Commercial Directory of the Jews of Gt. Britain.

HATTON GARDEN.

Goldberg, A., 2, Justice chambers; Master tailor.

ISLINGTON.

Henochsberg & Ellis, University House; Outfitters and contractors; and at Natal, Africa.
Karet, Moss, 34; Manager for Nathan & Co.

JOHN STREET, S.

Abrahams, P., 1; Master tailor.
Levy, Morris, 1; Master tailor.

KIRKDALE ROAD.

Ellenbogen, I., 161; House-furnisher and picture-frame manufacturer.
Ellenbogen, H., 138; Glass merchant.
Fagin, A., & Co., 109A–11–13; House-furnishing contractors.

WALTON ROAD.

Freudenstein, Nicolai, 49; Broker.
Hesselberg, D., 32; Draper, clothier, and general house-furnisher.
Schock, Hyman, 215; Glass and paint merchant.
Slefrig, I., 203; Glass merchant.

LIME STREET.

Phillips', 57; Wholesale watch manufacturers, jewellers, and silversmiths.
Robinson, Ralph, 23; Manufacturer of cigars, and tobacconist.

LIVERPOOL.

Commercial Directory of the Jews of Gt. Britain.

London Road.

Berliner Bros., 88, Kempston Street ; Master tailors.
Fink, Simon ; Master tailor for Beaty Bros.
Lipson, Jac., and Lipkin, Rt., 100–2 ; and 7, Hart Street ; Liverpool Furnishing Co.
Samuel Bros., 98 ; London drapers, etc.
Stern, Isidor, 212 ; Crown Furnishing Co.

Lord Street.

Benas, L., & Son, 1 ; Bankers and bullion dealers.
Isaac, J. N., 25 ; Solicitor.
Robinson, 24, N. John Street ; Solicitor.

Manchester Street.

Aronsberg, M., 40 ; Optician.
Levy Barnard, 4 ; Watchmaker and jeweller.
Matthews, David, 14 ; St. John's bazaar, grocers' factor, office and shop-fitter.
Pestka, J., 10 ; Master tailor.

Mill Street.

Urdang Bros., Bran Street; South End cabinet works; Speciality in bedroom suites.

Monument Place.

Myers & Co. ; Clothiers.

Moss Street.

Marcus, Theodore (trading as T. Marcus & Co.), 4 ; House-furnishers and upholsterers.

LIVERPOOL.

Commercial Directory of the Jews of Gt. Britain.

Mulberry Street.
Silverstein, I., 23 ; Tailor for the trade.

Netherfield Road.
Dolowich, N., 29 ; Glass merchant.

Norton Street.
Solomons, Lazarus, 40 ; Tailor and waterproof-garment maker.
Steinberg, S., 44 ; Master tailor.

Old Hall Street.
Liebeschutz, A., & Son; 60–62 ; General merchants.
Zagury, African Chambers ; Cotton merchant.

Paradise Street.
Goldberg Bros. 43 ; Pipe manufacturers.
Goldson, H., 39A ; Outfitting.
Moss & Co ; House-furnishers.

Park Lane.
Cohen, A., 50 ; Clothier, bullion dealer, and passenger agent.
Cohen, Jonas M., 91–95–97 ; Wholesale and retail clothing and outfitting stores.
Pool, Abm., 63 ; Clothier and outfitter.

Park Place.
Mosses H., 24 ; House-furnisher and insurance agent.

LIVERPOOL.
Commercial Directory of the Jews of Gt. Britain.

Park Road.
Friedman, J., 72 ; Custom tailor and draper.
Urdang, S. H., 157–159 ; Picture-frame manufacturer.

Pembroke Place.
Aaron, S., 27, Hardwick Street ; Master tailor.
Abrahams, Jac., 33 ; Wholesale cabinet maker.
Auerbach ; House-furnisher.
Gold, A., 12, Stand Street ; Jeweller.
Grant's Globe Furnishing Co.
Lipson & Lipkin, 7 and 9 ; Alexandra Furnishing Co.
Rosenbloom, S., 50A ; Master tailor.
Shock, S., 104 ; House-furnisher.
Silverman, M., 17, Hardwick Street : General draper, clothier, and house-furnisher.
Torlowsky, Reuben, 6, Hardwick Street ; General draper clothier, and furniture dealer.

Pleasant Street.
Coopar, Morris, 40 ; Master tailor.
Kofski, A., 49 ; Master tailor.

Prescott Street.
Beck, M., 10 ; Wholesale cigarette manufacturer.

Prince's Road.
Friedeberg, Rev. S. ; Min. Heb. congregation.

Ranelagh Street.
Jacob's ; Woollen merchants.
Lewis's ; Merchants.
Romain, S. A., 7 (place) ; Jeweller.

LIVERPOOL.

Commercial Directory of the Jews of Gt. Britain.

Renshaw Street.

Lazarus, Judah, 63 ; Family butcher and poulterer.
Morris' G., 57 ; Cigar and tobacco dealer.

Richmond Row.

Salomon, M., 92-94-96 ; General house-furnisher.

Rodney Street.

Siemms, A. I. D., Prof., 76 ; Chiropodist. Est. 1834.

Rupert Hill.

Cohen, L., 45 ; Draper.
Goldberg, E., 43 ; Draper and clothier.

Russell Street.

Cohen, M., 66 ; Dealer in tailors' trimmings.
Fleeter, Sol., 38, Warren Street ; Master tailor.
Goldstein, M., 76 ; Family butcher, poulterer, etc.
Jacobson, Jos., 15A, Edward Street; Wholesale clothier.
Klompus, S., 25, Warren Street ; Trousers manfr.
Levy, Herman, 46, Warren Street ; Manager of coat department for Lyons & Co.
Phillips, M., Mrs., 35 ; Select private and commercial boarding house.
Swift, J., 1 ; Family butcher, poulterer, etc.

Sankey Street.

Abrahamson, R., 3 ; Emigrant outfitter and money exchange.

Scotland Road.

Ginsburg, A., 97-99 ; General house-furnisher and bedstead and bedding manufacturer.

LIVERPOOL.

Commercial Directory of the Jews of Gt. Britain.

Harrinson, L., 319 and 323; Draper, clothier, and general outfitter.
Perlovitch, J., 334; and 46, Kirkdale Road, and 37, Stanley Road; Furnisher and picture-frame manfr.

Seymour Street.
Robinson, A. B., L.D.S., 29; Dental surgeon.
Sherowitz, Harris, 49; Manchester warehouseman.

Smith Street.
Lappin, S. J., 88; House-furnisher.

Soho Street.
Fagin, M,, 106; Furniture dealer.

Spencer Street.
Baker, M., 7; General warehouseman.

St. Anne Street.
Davidson, H., 102; Glass merchant.
Levy, Abm., 12–14; House-furnisher and importer of mouldings and picture-frame manufacturer.
Robinson, Henry, 13; Importer of German and French mouldings and frame manufacturer.
Solomon & Co., 37; Importers of German mouldings, etc.

St. James Street.
Tvergo, Jos., 92A, and 3, Duncan Street; Wholesale cabinet maker.

St. John's Lane.
Marcus, B., 11; Jeweller.

Vine Street.
Aronsberg, N., 134; Wine and vinegar manufacturer.

LIVERPOOL.

Commercial Directory of the Jews of Gt. Britain.

WALTON.

Kreps, O., 28, County Road ; Draper.

WATER STREET.

Edwards, M. H., 5, Back Goree ; Emigration agent and outfitting stores.

Hart, N. S., 52, Tower Bridge ; Loan office.

WHITECHAPEL.

Solomon, L., 24 ; Office fitter. Est. 1851.

WILLIAMSON STREET.

Bernfeld, J., 20 ; Master tailor.
Lazarus, I., 16 ; Master tailor.

BOOTLE.

Barnett, M., 220, Rimrose Road ; Furnisher.

Bernstein, H. M., 34–34½, Derby Road ; Picture-frame maker and fancy goods dealer.

Black, Isaac, 66, Stanley Road ; Cabinet maker and upholsterer.

Cohen, David M., 308, Derby Road ; Clothier and outfitter.

Goldman, 19, Peel Road ; General draper, clothier, and jeweller.

Goldstein, N., 104, Strand Road : Glass merchant.

Gorfunkle, Saml., 50, Stanley Road ; Complete house-furnisher, upholsterer, and bedding manufacturer.

Morris, M., 131, Bedford Road ; Salesman.

Norris, J. L., 41–43, Stanley Road ; Clothier and outfitter.

Swift, H., & Sons, 284, Stanley Road ; Complete house-furnishers.

LONDON.
Commercial Directory of the Jews of Gt. Braitin.

ALDGATE.

GOODMAN'S FIELDS, E.

Fifer, N. & Co., 6, Tenter Buildings, St. Mark Street Whosesale boot, shoe & slipper manufacturer.

Isaacs, Simon, 6, Great Alie Street; Baker and confectioner, for weddings, balls and parties; Passover provisions.

Jacobs & Co., Passover cake baker.

Shapero, P., 49, Gt. Alie Street; Wholesale & retail Hebrew and English bookseller; Passover spirits and wine.

GREAT PRESCOT STREET, E.

Abrahams, R. & Co., 25; Wholesale and export boot and shoe manufacturers; Established 1886.

Bonn, Jos., 12; Hotel and restaurant. Bonn's magnificent suite of rooms for weddings, confirmations, balls and general entertainments; Est. 1870.

Cohen, B. S.; Pencil Manufacturer.

Wolf & Co., 14; Passover Cake assn.

HOUNDSDITCH, E.C.

Cohen, A., 157; Restaurant. Late of Hatton Garden.

Swaebe, Daniel, 135; Family Butcher; Smoked and salt beef, worsht, sausages, &c.

KING & MITRE STREETS, E.C.

Phillps, Ph. & Co.,; Fruit and cokernut merchants. Telegraphic address: "Cokernut, London."

LEMAN STREET, E.

Cohen, A., 82; Ostrich-feather manufacturer.

Cohen, J., 4, Little Alie Street; Wholesale hat and cap manufacturer.

LONDON

Commercial Directory of the Jews of Gt. Britain.

Fordonski, M., 33 ; India-rubber, waterproof clothing manufacturer. And at Bancroft Rd. Est. 1868.
Goldman, H., 37 ; Builder and house-decorator, plumber, gas and hot-water fitter. Estimates. Est. 1887
Makover, W. & G. 28 ; Wholesale and retail woolen merchants and dealers in job lots and cap stuffs.
Newman, M., 63 ; Hand-sewn boot and shoe maker for custom trade.
Passes, G., 47 ; Draper and General Dealer.
Rubenstein, B., 45 ; Jeweller. Also tobacconist and cigar dealer. Hall for weddings.
Van Praagh, A., 14, St. Mark Street ; Monumental mason. Works : Baron Sclater Street.

Mansell Street, E.

Freedman, J. & Co., 15 ; Manufacturers plain and fancy card boxes. Cigarette, drug and chemical boxes a speciality.
Jacobs, S., 43 ; Custom tailor.
Moses, S., 65 ; Government stores dealer.
Rutkowski, Lipman A., 14 ; Woollen merchant, warehousman and stock buyer. Est. 1885.

Middlesex Street, E.C.

Abrahams, A., 31 ; Wholesale and retail provision merchant. Est. 150 years. Telegraphic address : " Phantasmas." Telephone No. 11054.
Barnett, S., 91 ; Wholesale and retail provision merchants.
Dubowski, B. & Sons, 48 ; Wholesale & retail grocers, provision merchants, Italian warehousemen and mineral water manufacturers. Branches : 106 and 73, Brick Lane, 22 and 138, Wentworth Street, and 47, Commercial Road. Est. 1880.

LONDON.

Commercial Directory of the Jews of Gt. Britain.

Green, J., 26; Wholesale boot, shoe and slipper manufacturer for home and export. Est. 1879.

Hart, Bodger, 69; Fresh and fried fishmonger and smoked salmon merchant. Est. 50 years.

Hyams, D., 51; Wholesale & retail dealer in English and foreign pickles and provisions. Orders for Passover received. Matzos supplied.

Krotoski, A., 67; Family butcher, poulterer, worsht and smoked and salt beef dealer.

Litman, F. & Co., 64; General dealers, woollen drapers and job buyers of all kinds of fancy woollen goods. Est. 1886.

NEW CASTLE STREET, E.C.

Jacobs, M. & J., 16; Wholesale clothing manufacturers for home and export. Est. 1889.

OLD CASTLE STREET, E.C.

Lipman, Isaac, 112; Wholesale and retail wall-paper merchant. Contracting painter and white-washer. Factory and warehouse job lots bought.

ST. MARY AXE, E.C.

Isac, Moise B., 58; Oriental Carpet Merchant.

Jacobs & Artinoff, 71–73; Society for advertising in the Ottoman empire and elsewhere. And at 60, Commission Han, Galata, Constantinople.

Jacobs, H. & Co., 71–73, Manufacturers of every description of filters, glass, china, &c., and general merchants. And at Constantinople.

Moss, J. & Co., 56; Japan and China Merchants.

LONDON.

Commercial Directory of the Jews of Gt. Britain.

STONEY LANE, E.C.

Silver, H. & E., 10a; Caterers, cooks & confectioners. Country orders received.

WENTWORTH STREET, E.C.

Boam, J., 118 & 119; Wholesale and retail piece broker, trimming and general dealer.

Bonn, Joseph, 2; Caterer, cook and confectioner. Wedding breakfasts, dejeuners, &c. Orders by post punctually attended to. Est. 1860.

Dubowsky, A., 130; Wholesale and retail family grocer and provision dealer. Passover provisions and groceries. Branch: 65, Commercial Street.

Freedman, A., 27a; Buyer and seller of ladies' wardrobes, &c.

Levy, Mark, 144; English and foreign fruiterer. Established 1864.

Matthews, M., 131; Wholesale and retail clothier and juvenile outfitter. Est. 1886. Branches: 2a, Stoney Lane, and 93, Wentworth Buildings.

LONDON.

Commercial Directory of the Jews of Gt. Britain.

Aldgate Avenue, E.

Barnett, W., 1 ; Electric goods dealer.
Bloomberg, F. N., 1 ; Shoe manufacturer.
Burstein, M. & Co., 12 ; Cigarette manufacturers.
Cohen, M. & Co., 9 ; Shoe manufacturers.
Finkelson & Co., 5 ; Boot and shoe manufacturers.
Goldhill, A., 1 ; Sponge importer.
Israel, J. A., 8 ; Agent.
Leapman, D. & Co., 12 ; Wholesale clothiers.
Lewin & Co., 10 ; Boot and shoe manufacturers.
Polish Young Men's Entertainment Society, 7.
Posner & Co., 9 ; Cap manufacturers.
Sommers, J. & Co., 5 ; Boot manufacturers.
Weitzman, 7 ; Card-box manufacturer.

Camomile Street, E.C.

Franck, S. M., 25 ; Japan and China merchants.
Isaacs, Alfred & Sons, 16 ; Wholesale Stationers and engravers.

Aldersgate Street, E.C.

Eilenberg & Zeltner, Edmund's Buildings ; Manufacturers of India-rubber goods.
Felsenstein Bros., Edmund's Buildings ; Wholesale furriers.
Greenberg and Sons, 3, Manchester Avenue ; Leather and glue merchants.
Keyzor, Baron J., 157 ; Wholesale clock manufacturer and importer.
Kosminsky, S., 170 ; Wholesale furrier.
Levy, J. and Son, 135 ; Wholesale furrier.

A

LONDON.

Commercial Directory of the Jews of Gt. Britain.

Newman, H. M. & Co., Limited, 69 ; Importers and manufacturers of cigars and snuff.
Rubenson, S., 11, Edmund's Place ; Manufacturing furrier and skin merchant.
Simmons, A. & Co., 34 ; Wholesale furriers.
Woolf, J., 190 ; Wholesale furrier.

AUSTIN FRIARS, E.C.

Mocatta, A. and Co., 22 ; Stock and share brokers.

BARBICAN.

Woolf Bros., 37 ; Wholesale tailors.

BEECH STREET.

Arthur, H., 45 ; Bespoke tailor.
Figur & Cohen, 2 ; Furriers.
Moss, D., 3 ; Glass and China merchant.
Ramus, S., 38 ; Ostrich feather manufacturer.

CHISWELL STREET.

Guttmann, M. & Co., 14 ; Manufacturer of embroidery.
Herz and Co., 14 ; Manufacturer of embroidery.
Herzberg, B. & Co., 11 ; Felt hat manufacturers.
Lion, Lion & Son, 32 ; Wholesale and export boot and shoe manufacturers.
Loewenstein & Hecht, Moor Lane ; Merchants.
Rosenthal Bros., 14 ; Blouse, shirt and jersey manufs.

BATTERSEA.

Goldman, S., 51, Northcote Road ; Dental surgeon and chiropodist.
Levy, S., 222, Battersea Park Rd. ; House-furnisher.
Morris, M., 3, Northcote Road ; House-furnisher.

LONDON.

Commercial Directory of the Jews of Gt. Britain.

BAYSWATER.

Hirsch, A. & Co., 15, Hereford Road; Family grocer and provision dealer, olive and frying oil merchant. Passover provisions. Est. 1872.

Marks, Chas., Ledbury Road; Fish merchant. Established 1878.

Rubenstein, I., 26, Richmond Road; Ladies' and gentlemen's tailor and habit-maker.

BELL LANE, SPITALFIELDS.

Esterson, S., 19; Hebrew and English teacher, bookseller and dealer silk and woollen talaisim, &c.

BETHNAL GREEN.

Cohen, W., 92, Green Street; Linen draper, hosier and haberdasher. Also master tailor.

Finkelstein, J., 26, Hare Street; Wholesale boot and shoe manufacturer.

Goldberg & Bloom, 31-33, Hare Street; New and second-hand furnishers. Factory for bedroom suite manufactory—6, Bacon Street.

Hanreck, H. M., 117; Surgeon & mechanical dentist.

Jacobs, Lazarus, 113, Green Street; Merchant tailor and juvenile outfitter. And at 485, Cambridge Rd.

Jacobs. Woolf, 161, Cambridge Road; Family butcher and poulterer, smoked beef, sausages, &c.

Kairys, P., 6, New Nichol Street; General cabinet and bedroom suite and toilet pedestal manufacturer. Established 1885.

Kaplan, N., 32, Columbia Road; Wholesale and retail bedroom furniture manufacturer.

Lenz, Morris, 95, Green Street: Linen draper, hosier and haberdasher. Est. 1889.

LONDON.

Commercial Directory of the Jews of Gt. Britain.

Nathan ; Gassfitter, plumber, etc.

Moses, S., 449, Green Street ; Boot and shoe manuf.

Norden, Louis, 13, Columbia Road ; Frame maker and upholsterer to the trade.

Phillips, Hy., 25, Green Street ; Leather seller and general job buyer. Est. 1880.

Polinski, H., 26, Columbia Road ; General bedroom furniture manufacturer.

Praeger, A., 2-4, Fountain Street, Virginia Road ; Wholesale and export boot and shoe manuf. Established 1883.

Sandground, L., 4, Club Row ; Bedroom suite, sideboard, duchesse toilet-table, writing-table, and general cabinet maker.

Solomon, H., 60, Columbia Road ; Bedroom suite, duchesse toilet and washstand, pedestal toilet and writing tables manufacturer. Retail housefurnisher, 61, Brick Lane.

Solomon, M., 30, Columbia Road ; General bedroom furniture manufacturer to the trade. Est. 1887.

Zimbler, J., Green Street ; Boot and shoe manuf.

BEVIS MARKS, E.C.

Levin, M. L., Importer of beads for African trade.

BILLITER STREET, E.C.

Rosenfeld, A. and Co., 18 ; Colonial merchant.

BISHOPSGATE.

Bowman, Isaac, 27, Steward Street ; Custom tailor.

Cohen, D. H. and Co., 15, Windsor Street ; Tin-plate merchants.

LONDON.

Commercial Directory of the Jews of Gt. Britain.

Franklin, J. & Son, 58 to 61, White Lion Street; Wholesale and export boot and shoe manufacturers. Est. 1870.

Joseph, David & Co., 108; Timber merchant.

Lazarus, R. & Son, 86; Government store contractors.

Magnus, Oscar, 6, Steward Street; Grocer.

Nathan, J., 6 and 11, Artillery Passage; Family butcher and poulterer. And 105, High Road, Kilburn, and 187, Mile End Road.

Phillips, Coleman, 3, Steward Street; Family grocer and Passover provisions.

Rosenbaum, Henry, 65; and 20-22, Brushfield Street; Woolen draper.

Rosenthal, Mark; Furrier.

Wartski, B. & Son, 78-79; Waterproof garment manufacturers to the Prince of Wales.

Woolf, J. & Co, 37, Steward Street; Wholesale and export boot and shoe manufacturers. Est. 1858.

BLOOMFIELD STREET, E.C.

Goldstein, D., 5; Restaurant. Est. 1858.

BLOOMSBURY.

Hyman, J., jun., 14-21, High Street; Clothier and outfitter.

Bow, E.

Polack, B. S., Lincoln House, Lincoln Street; Monumental mason, West Ham. Works: Gough Road, Stratford. Adjoining Jews' cemetery.

Rose, B, 196, Roman Road; Watch and clock maker and jeweller to the trade. Est. 1887.

LONDON.
Commercial Directory of the Jews of Gt. Britain.

BURDETT ROAD, E.

Raphael, H. L., Thomas Street; Gold and silver refiner.

CALEDONIA ROAD.

Rosenberg, G. W., 42; Merchant tailor and outfitter. Est. 1874.

Solomons, Alfred, 195; Builders' and plumbers' supply stores.

CAMDEN TOWN.

Benjamin, B., 133, High Street; City Clothing Co.

Jones, A., 117, High Street; Merchant tailor and outfitter.

CANNING TOWN.

BARKING ROAD.

Bernstein, Mrs. S., 266; Herbalist.

Morris, W.; Watchmaker and jeweller.

VICTORIA DOCK ROAD.

Alvarez, H., 2; Clothier.
Bleiberg, S., 108; Draper and hosier.
Davis, J., 17; China and glass dealer.
Levy, 64; Boot and shoe dealer.
Marks, B., 66; Dealer in china, glass, and fancy goods.
Moses; Clothier and tailor.
Nathan, J., 90; Clothier and jeweller.

CANONBURY, N.

Abrahamson & Arnold, 2, Monte Cristo Parade; Complete house-furnishers, bedstead, bedding and upholstery works.

LONDON.

Commercial Directory of the Jews of Gt. Britain.

Flatau, A. 24, Newington Green Road ; Wardrobe dealer.
Freedman, A. (*of Swansea*), 131, Grosvenor Road : Merchant.
Grossberg, M., 108, Matthias Road ; Custom tailor.
Jacobs, J., 67, Newington Green Road ; Butcher.
Rose, Isidor, 95, Green Lanes ; " La Rose " high art photographic studio.
Salomons, Mrs. B., 8, Ferntower Road ; Grocer.
Schaap, L., 9, Ferntower Road ; Embroider, silk "talaisim" and Hebrew bookseller, etc.
Van Abbe, 93, Green Lanes ; Family butcher.
Wolfsbergen, I. L., 10, Ferntower Road ; Butcher.

CAREY STREET, W.C.

Raphael, L. S., 3, New Court ; Barrister.
Rosenthal, L. H., 8, New Court ; Barrister.

CHARING CROSS ROAD.

Moss, Isaac, 95 ; Clothier and outfitter. Est. 1888.
Steinberg, G. S., 100 ; Master tailor. Est. 1883.

CHEAPSIDE, E.C.

Meyers, J. and H., 150 ; Wholesale furriers.
Rosenthall and Co., 63, Friday Street ; Wholesale furriers.
Solomons, A., and Co., 32, Bread Street ; Wholesale furriers.

CLAPHAM, S.

Marks, Henry ; Merchant.

CLERKENWELL.

Bowman, H. and Co., 159, Goswell Road ; Wholesale and retail clothiers. And at 5A, Percival Street.

LONDON.

Commercial Directory of the Jews of Gt. Britain.

Segal, D., 69, Myddelton Street; Diamond mounter and setter to the trade. Country orders.

COLEMAN STREET, E.C.

Tuck, Raphael & Sons; Art publishers for home and export.

COMMERCIAL ROAD, E.

Annenberg, I., 273; The "Non Plus Ultra" waterproof clothing manufacturer.
Barnstein, S. & Son; 14, Philpot Street; Wholesale shoe and slipper manufacturers. Est. 1885.
Cohen, G. Sons & Co., 600; Iron merchants.
Cohen, H., 160 and 134; Tailors' trimmings.
Cohen, Ph. & Co., 26; Wholesale ironmongers.
Franklin, S., 21; Boot and shoe manufacturer.
Harris & Sons, 84-86; Tobacconists.
Harris, L., 53; Watchmaker and jeweller.
Harris, N., 476; Merchant tailor and outfitter.
Klein, L., 52, Greenfield Street; High-class tailor and outfitter and dealer in woollens. Special quotations to privates.
Lerner, S., 137, Back Church Lane; Family grocer. Passover provisions and groceries supplied. By ecclesiastical authority.
Lion Bros., 24; Wholesale clothiers.
Moses, Abm., 132; Master tailor; Reliance Deposit and Loan Co., Ltd.
Rosenberg, M., 59, Umberston Street; Wholesale and retail baker.
Samuels, Morris, 471; Merchant tailor and juvenile outfitter. Est. 1885.
Schleifstein, A., 275; Wholesale and retail woollen fancy goods, hosiery, etc. And at 11, Stoney Lane.

LONDON.

Commercial Directory of the Jews of Gt. Britain.

Sichel, M., 105; Umbrella and stick maker, tobacconist and news agent; London and New York Jewish publications.
Wolff, Isaac, 150; Hairdresser, perfumer, and chiropodist.
Yaffe, Louis, 120, Back Church Lane; Family grocer and upholsterer. Passover groceries supplied.

COMMERCIAL STREET.

Angel, C., 130; Importers of mouldings, lithographers, etc.
Barnett, G., 85; Wholesale boot and shoe manfacturer.
Bender, E., 45; Plumber and gasfitter.
Bodansky, Mrs., 81; French milliner.
Brandon, J., 79; Tobacconist.
Brezinsky, H. & Co., 50, Wentworth Street; Wholesale baby-linen manufacturers and warehousemen.
Cohen, D., 55; Confectioner.
Cohen, M., Puma Court; Mantle manufacturer.
Greenfield, W., 71; Wholesale Nougat manufacturer.
Guttwoch, C., cor. Wentworth; Woollen merchant.
Harris, M., 72; Baker.
Hart & Levy, 64; Wholesale clothiers.
Koenigsberg, H. & Son, 25; Wholesale furriers.
Langleben, H., 75; Clothier.
Levison, A., 49; Grocer.
Levy, M., 47; Sponge dealer.
London, L. & Sons, 10; Wholesale clothiers.
Ludski, B. & Sons, 63; Manufacturers of surgical instruments. Est. 1873.
Miller, L., 122; Clothier and outfitter.
Moses & Werkendam, 70; House-furnishers.
Moses, S. & Sons, 57; Importers of gilt mouldings.

LONDON.

Commercial Directory of the Jews of Gt. Britain.

Phillips, H. & Sons, 11 ; Wholesale clothiers.
Pool, E. S. & Co., 67 ; Woollen and trimmings merchants.
Reens, L. & Co., 59 ; Cigar manufacturers.
Silverstone, P. & Son, 149 ; Tailors and clothiers.
Shreider, L. & T., 57 ; Wholesale manufacturing furriers.
Weinstein, I., 77 ; Draper and hosier.
Zeigen Bros. & Co., 123 ; Cigar manufacturers.

SPITALFIELDS MARKET.
Wholesale Fruiterers.

Carn, I.	Joel, S.	Nickolls, M.
Cohen, A.	Joseph, I.	Rothschild, D.
Costa, A. de	Levy, Hy.	Solomons, H.
Costo, D. de	Levy, I.	Solomons, R.
Isaacs, H.	Mordecai, Z. & Sons.	Wehl & Tossell.
Israel, M.		Wolf, G.

COPTHALL AVENUE.

Cohen & Co., 4 ; Stockbrokers.
Moccata, M. Son & Browne, 24 ; Stockbrokers.

CORNHILL.

Guttman, Chas., 21 ; Merchant.
Keyser, A. & Co., 21 ; Foreign bankers.
Marks, A., 52 ; Manchester, London, and Midland Bank, Ltd.

LONDON.

Commercial Directory of the Jews of Gt. Britain.

COVENT GARDEN, W.C.

Wholesale Fruiterers.

Garcia, Jacobs & Co.	Jacobs, E. & Sons.	Nathan, Joe. Phillips, A.
Harris, L.	Jacobs, L.	Phillips, A., Jr.
Isaacs, A.	Jacobs, S. G.	Solomon, E.
Isaacs Bros.	Kauffman, I.	Solomon, I.
Isaacs, M.	Kauffman, Mrs.	Woolf & Jacobs.
Isaacs, Saml.	Levy, H.	
Israel & Joel.	Nathan, J.	

Simsohn, S., 38, Russell Street; Wholesale Florist. Est. 1888.

CRIPPLEGATE.

Rothschild, S., 11, Silk Street; Foreign agent.

CURTAIN ROAD, E.C.

Barnett, Phillip, 94-96; General turner and carver, square and oval turning, fret-cutting and cornice-pole manufacturer.

Clozenberg & Son, 119; Wholesale and export cabinet and looking-glass manufacturers and timber merchants.

Cohen, B. & Sons; Wholesale and export cabinet manufacturers.

Jacobs, E. & Co., 129; Bedding manufacturers.

Jacobs, H. & Son, 73, Scrutton Street; Wholesale and export furniture manufacturers and upholsterers.

Joseph, John, 34, Great Eastern Street; Drawing and dining-room chair and couch manufacturer.

LONDON.

Commercial Directory of the Jews of Gt. Britain.

Kohn & Josef, 54, Great Eastern Street; Furnishers.

Lazarus, H. & Son, 33; Manufacturers brass and iron bedsteads and bedding and iron safes.

Levy, George J., 60, Great Eastern Street; Wholesale cabinet maker and upholsterer.

Marks, George, 131; Wholesale and retail looking-glass and cabinet manufacturer and upholsterer.

Sandground, D., 17, Phipps Street; Hardwood bedroom suite and sideboard manufacturer.

CUTLER STREET, HOUNDSDITCH.

Greenholtz, H., 32; Manufacturing furrier. A select stock of furs always on hand. Gentlemen's fur-lined coats a specialty. Est. 1881.

DUKE STREET, E.C.

Britton, L. A. & Sons, 46; Wholesale and retail oil and provision merchants.

Cohen, M., 26; Merchant tailor.

Cooper, Woolf, Opposite to Great Synagogue; Wholesale and retail Hebrew bookseller.

Gollancz, A.; Wholesale jeweller.

Hyams, H. H., 8; Insurance agent and Secretary Bread, Meat, and Coal Charity. Institution for Relief of the Indigent Blind. Jewish Ladies' Benevolent Loan Society. Office Jews' College.

Jacobs and Co., 12-14; Bookbinders.

Kepelonsky, Schwartz and Co., 20; Tobacconists.

Levinton, M. H., 8 : Solicitor.

Levy, A., 17; Carman.

Levy, S., 30; Tailor; also for the trade.

LONDON.

Commercial Directory of the Jews of Gt. Britain.

Lyons, H., 39 ; Orange dealer.
Pehr, M. and Co., 35 ; Cigarette manufacturers.
Romain, M., 21 ; Jeweller.
Rosenbaum, Henry, 5 ; Woollen draper.
Silver, I. and Son, 15 ; Confectioners.
Woolf, I. and Co. ; Boot manufacturers.
Zagury, A., 18 ; Merchant.

Edgeware Road, W.

Emanuel, J., 21, Chapel Street (the only address) ; Fruiterer and purveyor of vegetables. Est. 1885.
Lazarus, R. & Sons, 225 ; Cycle and athletic stores.
Lyons, J., 36 ; Hairdresser.
Lyons, S., 36 ; Insurance agent.
Simmons, Jos., 260 ; General complete outfitters.
Woolf, B. S. & Co., 294 ; Clothiers and outfitters.

Euston Square.

Levien, Louis, 92, Seymour Street ; Cook and confectioner. Tables, seats, plate, cutlery china, glass, etc., lent on hire. Est. 1853.

Farringdon Road, E.C.

Levy, S. J. & Co., 71 ; Optical and photographic warehouse.
Wanzer & Defries, 101 ; Patent Safety Lamp Manufacturing Co., Ltd.

Finsbury Circus, E.C.

Emanuel, Lewis, 36 ; Solicitor.

LONDON.

Commercial Directory of the Jews of Gt. Britain.

FINSBURY SQUARE, E.C.

Cohen, Sol., 15, South Street; Wholesale furrier.
Flatau, Christopher Street; Ostrich feather dresser.
Jacobs, P. and Son, 7, Sun Street; Glass and china merchants.
Joseph, C. & Co., 10, South Street; African merchants.
Leibler, H., 9, Christopher Street; Custom tailor.
Lyons, H., 34, Clifton Street; Picture-frames, etc.
Rosenthal, S., 6, Christopher Street; Electrician.
Zimmer, 10, Sun Street; Gold-foil merchant.

FITZROY SQUARE, W.

Rosenthal, J. and Co., 23, Southampton Street; Silversmiths.

FORE STREET, E.C.

Arnholz, A., 78; Cigar importer and tobacconist.
Besels, J., 14; Importer and manufacturer of foreign and lined-work baskets.
Brager, J., 82; Fancy leather goods merchant.
Cohen, S. & Co.; Waterproof clothing manufacturers.
Davis, M. and Son, 94; Warehousemen and silk merchants.
Emanuel, Max, 83; Manufacturer French china, trinket sets, vases, etc.
Frankel, S. (& Sons), 115; Skin and woollen merchants.
Hatschek, Louis and Co., 10; Vienna fancy goods merchants.
Hecht, E., 108, 109; Trimming and button importer.
Hirsch Bros., 168, 109; Manufacturers fancy leather goods.
Moser Bros., 46; China and glass manufacturers.
Myers and Co., 102; Belgian glass importers.
Nathan and Co., 102; Merchants.

LONDON.

Commercial Directory of the Jews of Gt. Britain.

Nussbaum, J., 46 ; Wholesale and export umbrella-stick manufacturer.
Rosenthal, Aaronson and Co., 96 ; Merchants.
Wiener, L., 91 ; Wurtemberg Electro-plate Co.

GOLDEN LANE, E.C.

Rosenstein and Lewis, 27, Playhouse Yard ; Piece-brokers and general dealers, and buyers and sellers of leather cuttings, etc.

GREAT MARSHALL STREET, W.

Solomon, J. I., 55 ; Solicitor.

GREAT PULTENEY STREET, SOHO.

Klovonski, S., 13 ; Master tailor. Est. 1883.
Solomons, Sol., 24 ; Master and custom tailor. Established 1863.
Solomons, S. W., 24 ; Master and custom tailor. Est. 1887.
Sick Benefit Society *(temporary)*, George Hotel, Great St. Andrew Street, W. ; S. Simsohn, President ; M. Schwarzberg, Vice-President ; Alex. Chachkes, Treasurer ; M. Lazarus, Secretary.
West-End Evening Talmud Torah, 10, Green's Court ; J. Davis, President ; J. Victor, Vice-President ; M. Warshawski, Treasurer ; B. A. Fersht, Hon. Secretary ; M. Klein, Instructor.

GREAT WINCHESTER STREET.

Isaac, B., 22 ; Consul-General for Guatemala, S.A.

GREEK STREET, SOHO.

Velinski, Lewis, 55 ; Master tailor. Est. 1887.

HACKNEY ROAD.

Abrahams, A., 63 ; Merchant tailor.

LONDON.

Commercial Directory of the Jews of Gt. Britain.

Abrahams, I., 154, Goldsmith Row; General draper and hosier.
Barnett, H., 76; Lead, glass, and paper-hanging.
Blom, Nathan, 462; Importer of Havana and Mexican cigars and cigar manufacturer.
Green, J. M. & Son, 372; Boot and shoe manfrs.
Jacobs, D. & Son, 80 and 90; Bamboo furniture manfrs.
Jacobs, J., 70; House-furnisher.
Jacobs, S., 239; Shoe manufacturer.
Joseph, Bros., 29; Merchant tailors.
Kantrowitz, J., 266; Hairdresser and perfumer.
Kaplan, J., 158; Wholesale and export boot and shoe manufacturer. Factory: King's Place.
Kaufman, S. C., Green Street; Wholesale boot and shoe manufacturer.
Lewis, David, 230; Wholesale skin-rug manufacturer. Est. 1886.
Wallach, S., 351; Leather merchant.

HAMPSTEAD, S.

Barnett, L., M.D., 40, Broadhurst Gardens, S.W.

HOXTON.

Bloom, S., 212, Hoxton Street; Watch and clock maker, jeweller, electro-plater, and gilder.
Cohen, J. and Son, 157; Merchant tailors.
Cohen, P., 98; Tailor and draper.
Defries, W., 66; House-furnisher.
Isaacs, J., 90; Merchant tailor.
Isaacs, M., 108; Merchant tailor.
Kallis, I., 99; Clothier and outfitter.
Koleman, M., 113; Draper, etc.
Ornstein Bros., 47–79, Coronet Street; Wholesale manufacturing upholsterers and frame makers to the trade.
Samuels, A., 84; Merchant tailor.

LONDON.

Commercial Directory of the Jews of Gt, Britain.

Hackney Road.

Goldberg & Co., 412; Wholesale cap manufacturers.

Harris, S., 164; Dealer in Foreign and English provisions. Olives and cucumber a specialty.

Levy, S., 232; Furrier. Ladies' jacktes and trimmings made to order and repairs executed.

Pyzer, S., 300; Merchant tailor and outfitter.

Hammersmith.

Levy, J. M. 1a, Broadway Buildings, King street W., Merchant tailor.

Morris, I, 251-3-5, Hammersmith Road, W. House furnisher.

Pozner, J. 7-9, King street, W. General outfitter.

Hampstead Road, N.W.

Simons, J., 40. High-class tailor and outfitter.

Hatton Garden, E.C.

Cohen, J., 101; Restaurant. Weddings supplied.

English Optic Co., 35; Manufacturing opticians.

Harris & Co., 35; Diamond merchants.

Horwitz, D. & Co., 53; Wholesale opticians and manufacturers and importers of watchmakers' and jewelers' materials.

LONDON.

Commercial Directory of the Jews of Gt. Britain.

Isaacs, A. J., 44; Diamond merchant, dealer in precious stones, and manufacturing jeweler.

Jacobson, L., 85; Manufacturing jeweler, diamond mounter, carved ring maker, etc.

Jessel, E. J., 89; Diamond merchant and jeweler.

Keyzor, George B. & Co., 39; Importers of clocks, musical boxes and optical goods.

Kohn, Jos., 25. Diamond merchant.

Koritschoner, D., 23; Manufacturing diamond scales and all requisites for the diamond trade.

Laurence, Henry (Lionel Druiff), 44; Manufacturing optician.

Levenburgh, Moses, 52; General merchant.

Simmons, G. A., 90; Wholesale manufacturer meteorological instruments. Shipping and country orders.

Swaab, A., 13; Diamond merchant.

Wachmann, D., 14; Broker in rough and cut diamonds; colourer stones, pearls, etc.

Weigel, B., 35; Diamond mounter and jeweler.

Weiner, Samuel, 25a; Manufacturing jeweler.

Wolff & Reiss, 35; Diamond merchants.

LONDON.

Commercial Directory of the Jews of Gt. Britain.

Moses, M. H., 36; Wholesale clothier.
Moses, S. and Sons, 150; Wholesale clothiers.
Myers, B., 99; Complete house-furnisher; new and second-hand furnisher. Country dealers supplied. Est. 1826.
Myers, J., 104; George and Dragon.
Myers, S., 103; Printer.
Newmark, M., 55–56; Wholesale jeweller, watch manufacturer, fancy goods, etc.
Noar and Goldblum, 56; Fancy goods importer.
Phillips, L., 114; Wholesale clothier.
Samuel, M. and Co., 31; Shell box manufacturers, etc.
Samuel, M. S. and Co., 157; Watch manufacturers.
Simmons, J. and Co., 148; Oil and Italian warehousemen.
Singer, Max, 10, Stoney Lane; Agent and general warehouseman.
Spiers, M., 50; Wholesale clothier.
Spiers Bros., 50; Juvenile clothiers.
Vallentine and Son; Wholesale and retail stationers and booksellers and general printers.

ISLINGTON.

Hart, 34–36, High Street; Clothier and outfitter.
Henry, H. & Co., 175, Upper Street; Furriers.
Joseph, L., Balls Pond Road; Auctioneer and furnisher.
Langner Bros., 209, Balls Pond Road; General printers and stationers. Wedding and mourning stationery, engraving, etc.
Ritter, B., 17, Balls Pond Road; Wholesale and retail picture-frame and show-card manufacturer.
Siegenberg, L. and Son, 206, Upper Street; House-furnishers.

LONDON.

Commercial Directory of the Jews of Gt. Britain.

Silverstone, P. and Son, 288, Upper Street; Merchant tailors.
Snapper, Upper Street; Furrier.
Woolf, L. S., 41, High Street; Merchant tailor.

KENNINGTON PARK ROAD.

Joseph, Davies and Co., 6; Manufacturing opticians.

LEADENHALL, E.C.

Joseph and Bergel; Foreign bankers.

LEWISHAM.

Lancaster; High-class tailor and outfitter.

LIME STREET SQUARE.

Rosenheim, L. and Sons, 2; Wine shippers and merchants. And at 133, Lenai des Chartrois, Bordeaux.

LIVERPOOL STREET, E.C.

Elkan, J., 35 and 23; Jewelry and fancy goods.
Saqui and Lawrence; Fancy goods dealers.

LONDON ROAD, SOUTHWARK.

Aarons, L., 8 and 12; House-furnisher.
Chapman, Moss, 64, 65; The South London Tailor. Est. 1885.
Goldstein, Mrs. R.; Tobacconist.
Levy Bros., 60; Tobacconists and cigar importers.
Lyons, M., 3; House-furnisher.
Nathan, J., 125; Furnisher and antique dealer.
Silverston, R., 47; Clothier.
Simmons, Mrs. E.; Milliner.

LONDON.

Commercial Directory of the Jews of Gt. Britain.

LONDON WALL, E.C.

Cohen and Cohen, 72; Solicitors.
Kohn, Rudolph, 108; China and glass manufacturer.

LONG ACRE, W.C.

Simsohn, M., 137; Wholesale florist. Est. 1888.

MAIDA HILL, W.

Adelberg, M. V., 49, Shirland Road; Family butcher; Smoked and salt beef, wursht, sausages, etc. Est. 1860.
Rosenberg, H. and Sons, 51, Shirland Road; Purveyors of first-class poultry. Weddings, dinners, banquets, etc., supplied. Est. 1867. Telegraphic address: "Rosenberg," Shirland Road.

MARK LANE, E.

Kohn, A. S., 59; General merchant.
Rosenheim, Browne and Co., 59; Wholesale tea merchants.

MIDDLESEX STREET, E.C.

Abrahams, A., 31; Wholesale and retail provision merchant. Est. 150 years. Telegraphic address: "Phantasmas." Telephone No. 11054.
Barnett, S., 91; Wholesale and retail provision merchant.
Barnett, I., 87; Cheese factor, etc.
Blitz, A. H. and Co.; Poulterers.
Cohen, A.; Cook and confectioner.
Cohen, Mrs. A., 55; Ladies' wardrobes.
Cohen, I. and A.; Wholesale clothiers.
Dubowski, B. and Sons, 48; Wholesale and retail grocers, etc.
Green, J., 26; Wholesale boot, shoe, and slipper manufacturer for home and export. Est. 1879.

LONDON.

Commercial Directory of the Jews of Gt. Britain.

Harbour, S., 23 ; Milliner.
Hart, Bodger, 69 ; Fishmonger. Est. 50 years.
Hyams, D., 51 ; Pickles and provision dealer.
Hyman ; Provision dealer.
King, H., 21 ; Tailor.
Krotoski, A. (Successor to H. Samson), 67 ; Family butcher, poulterer, wursht & smoked & salt beef.
Littman, F. & Co., 64 ; General dealers, etc. Est. 1886.
Myers and Joseph, 68 ; Cooks and confectioners.
Nathan, P., 62 ; Friedfish dealer.
Prince, L., 54 ; Fancy goods dealer.
Silver, Mrs. M., 4 ; Confectioner.
Simmons, L., 19 ; Clothier.
Valentine, A., 49 ; Clothier.
Weber, W. and Sons, 18 ; Boot and shoe manfrs.
Woolf, I., 15 ; Milliner and stationer.

MILE END, E.

Abram, Alfred, 166 ; The Carlton warm baths ; hairdresser, perfumer, and cigar dealer. Est. 1880.
Alexander and Co., 234, Jubilee Street ; Wholesale hat and bonnet shape manufacturers.
Angel, A., 215, Jubilee Street ; Family butcher. Smoked and salt beef, wursht, and sausage manufacturer. Trade supplied. Est. 1886.
Bagel, A., 43, Raven Row ; Wholesale and export boot and shoe manufacturer.
Barnett, B., Cambridge Road ; Leather dealer.
Chissick and Co., 30 ; Wholesale and export boot, shoe, and slipper manufacturers.
Cohen, I., 266-270 ; Clothier and outfitter.
Hanreck, Lewis, 128 ; Hairdresser, perfumer, chiropodist, and surgical dentist.
Harris & Son, 1, Beaumont St. ; Monumental masons.

LONDON.

Commercial Directory of the Jews of Gt. Britain.

Hyman, O., 283 ; Tobacconist, etc.
Lazarus, L., 111 ; Cigar manufacturer and tobacconist.
Levene, P., 174 ; Watchmaker.
Levy, J., 48 ; Tailor and clothier.
Mordecai, Mark and Sons, 108 ; Importers of Havana and Mexican cigars and cigar manufacturers. Est. 1868.
Price, M., 482 ; General draper, etc.
Samuel, J. and Son, 147, Sydney Street ; Monumental masons and undertakers.
Siegenberg, J., Cannon Place ; Bedding manufacturer.
Simmons, A., 363 ; High-class bespoke tailor.
Tobins, J., 382 ; Watchmaker and jeweller.
Woolf, M., 93 ; Wholesale and retail skin merchant.

Milk Street, E.C.
Harfeld, Ellis, 5 ; Woollen merchant.

Milton Street, E.C.
Rosenthall and Co., 13, Chapel Street ; Blouse and fancy apron manufacturer.

Moorgate Street, E.C.
Raphael, Ralph, 59 ; Solicitor.

New Compton Street, Soho.
Kerstein, Morris, 70 ; Master and custom tailor and tailors' trimmings seller. Est. 1877.

Notting Hill, W.
Portnoi, Morris, 8, Bolton Road ; Master tailor for the trade.
Rosenbaum, H., 49, Pembridge Road ; Ladies' and gentlemen's tailor. Est. 1886.
Rosenfeld, Pizer, 126A, Portobello Road ; Bespoke tailor.

LONDON.

Commercial Directory of the Jews of Gt. Britain.

Shapiro, J., 57, Kensington Park Road ; Custom tailor and tailors' trimmings.
Vandyck, H., 20, Ladbroke Grove Road; Photographer.
White, L. E., 196, Portobello Road ; Family butcher.

Lancaster Road.

Sick Benefit Society ("Chevra Bikur Cholim"), 147 ; P. Rosenfield, President ; M. Portnoi, Vice-President; M. Greenberg, Treasurer; M. Middlevich, Secretary.

Oxford Street, W.C.

Goldberger, E., 231 (Oxford Circus Avenue); Wine agent.
Goldstein, Morris, 16, 18, and 20 ; Manufacturing jeweller. Sole proprietor of "The Chemical Diamonds."
Hyam and Co., Ltd., 114; Tailors, clothiers, etc. Also at Birmingham, Wolverhampton, and Leeds.
Joseph, Alex. ; Warehouse : Union Place, Wells Street ; and at 23, Bucknall Street.
Kosminski, M., 48, Berners Street; Wholesale furriers.
Mocatta, Benj. and Co., 37, Berners Street ; Music publishers.
Morris, Wm., 502 ; Jeweller.
Moses, M., 464 ; Jeweller.
Phillips, Benj., 438 ; Dealer in works of art.
Raphael, G., 7-9 ; Cigar manufacturer.
Raphael, J. and Co., 13 ; Wholesale opticians.
Samuel, Henry, 484 ; Dealer in works of art.
Samson, Saml.. 102 (W.) ; High-class ladies' tailor and mantle maker.
Wolff, Phillips and Co., 289 ; Cigar importers.
Wooff, I. 26, Berwick Street ; Master tailor.

LONDON.

Commercial Directory of the Jews of Gt. Britain.

PADDINGTON, W.

Frank, L. R., 300, Harrow Road; The Kosher Meat Company. Est. 1875.
White, L. E., 125, Harrow Road; Family butcher. Telegraphic address: "Pycnite," London. Telephone No. 7166.

PENTONVILLE ROAD.

Harris, J., 217; Fancy goods and draper.
Hyman, A., 260; Merchant tailor.
London, S., 182; Merchant tailor and outfitter.
Miller, M., 174; Custom tailor and master tailor for the trade.
Nathan, S., 214; Hatter.
Rosenberg, S., 265; Merchant tailor and outfitter. Est. 1874.
Simmons, Ellis, 238; Clothier and outfitter. Best second-hand and West-end misfits. Pattern cut for the wholesale trade. Founder of "London Cutlers' Trade Union," 1889.
Symonds and Co., 252; Tobacconists and cigar mfts.

PICCADILLY, W.

Hirsch, Baron, 82; Banker. Philanthropist.

POPLAR, CHRISP STREET.

Amstel, M., 9; Wholesale and retail tobacconist and foreign and domestic cigar dealer.
Davis, Sol., 69; Wholesale and retail China and glass dealer. Est. 1888.
Goldstein, Abm., 19; Wholesale and retail draper, and dealer in job lots and samples.
Marcus, Chas., 9a; Wholesale and retail draper and dealer in fancy goods.
Solomon, Graham, 83; Wholesale and retail general and fancy draper.

LONDON.

Commercial Directory of the Jews of Gt. Britain.

East India Dock.

Cassell & Co., 196 ; Manufacturers and importers of domestic appliances and musical instruments. Est. 1883.

Humphreys, L. and Co., 289 ; Wholesale and retail tobacco and cigar importer.

Leibow, P. M., 212 ; Pawnbroker, jeweller and clothier.

Portland Street, Soho.

King, S., 24 ; Wholesale and retail dealer in woollen rags and tailors' trimmings.

Warshawski, M., 25 ; Master tailor. Est. 1883.

Queen Victoria Street.

Kohn, Julius, Mansion House Chambers ; Sec. Imperial and Royal Austro-Hungarian Consulate-general.

Rosenthal, Adolphus and Co., 158 ; Paper agents and merchants.

Rothschild, Baron Alfred Charles de, Mansion House Chambers ; Hon. Austro-Hungarian Consul-gen.

Red Cross Street, E.C.

Jacobs, Lotheim and Co., 58 ; Wholesale manufacturing furriers.

Regent Street.

Rosenthal, H., 98 ; Aluminium manufacturer.

Royal Mint Street.

Rothschild, Alfred de ; Refiner.

LONDON.

Commercial Directory of the Jews of Gt. Britain.

REGENT STREET, W

Abrahams, M., 63, Beak Street; Family grocer and provision dealer. Passover groceries and provisions supplied. Established 1886.

Blumenthal, P., 28, Broad Street; Family grocer and provision dealer. Passover groceries supplied.

Bournstone, J., 3, West Street, Foubert's Place; Tailors' trimmings merchant, woollens, &c. Established 1888.

Chachkes, Alex., 54, Broad Street; General draper, hosier, and fancy goods draper.

Davis, Joel, 9, Green's Court; Family butcher and poulterer. Smoked beef, sausages, &c. Est. 1878.

Goldstein, Mrs. J., 43, Marshall Street; Family grocer and English and Foreign provisions. Passover provisions supplied.

Gottlieb, Levy, 2, Edward Street; Family butcher, poulterer, smoked beef, sausages, &c.

Honigman Bros, 35, Lexington Street; Family grocers and provision dealers. Passover provisions supplied.

King, Samuel, 24, Portland Street; Wholesale and retail dealer in woollen rags & tailors' trimmings.

Laventhal, L. and Sons, Poland Street; Drapers.

Rupinski, H., 18, Broad Street; Master tailor.

Segenfield, J., 4, Ganton Street; Tobacconist and foreign and domestic cigar and cigarette manufacturer.

Solcberg, Gustav, 45, Lexington Street; West-end restaurant, caterer for weddings and parties.

ST. GEORGE'S EAST.

Jacobs, Jos., 77; Wholesale surgical instrument manufacturer. Established 1887.

LONDON.

Commercial Directory of the Jews of Gt. Britain.

St. John's Wood.

Herschman, W., 107, Boundary Road; English and foreign provision store. Passover provisions. Agent for Jacob's Oil and Abraham's smoked beef, &c. Established 1883.

St. Luke's.

Franks, A. H. and Son, 63, Old Street; Tobacco, cigar and cigarette manufacturers.
Hirshberg, L. D., 257, Old Street; Watch and clock maker, Jeweller and optician. Established 1886.

St. Paul's.

Lange & Co., 2, Godliman Street; Furriers.
Meyers & Co., 31; Wholesale Furriers.

St. Swithin's Lane.

Rothschild, N. M. & Sons, New Court; Bankers.

Shadwell.

Aarons, J., 19 & 42, King David Lane; Bespoke tailor and outfitter. Established 1883.

Shaftesbury Avenue.

Redstone, Morris, 198; Linen draper, hosier, and fancy goods merchant.
Victor, J., 161; Bespoke tailor, outfitter, and habit maker. Established 1887.

Southwark Street, E.C.

Rosenfeld & Co., The Exchange, Hop Merchants.

LONDON.

Commercial Directory of the Jews of Gt. Britain.

SPITALFIELDS.

BELL LANE.

Cohen, M. & Co., 11; Wholesale and retail grocers, provision and fish and oil dealers. Passover provisions at 19, Brady Street, Whitechapel.

Esterman, S., 19; Hebrew and English teacher, bookseller and dealer in silk & woollen "talaisim" &c.

Lissack. M. S., 8 (opposite to Free School); Family butcher, smoked & salt beef, worsht, sausages, &c.

CRISPIN STREET.

Smith, A. W., 4; Butcher and poulterer. Smoked and salt beef, &c. Dealer in all kinds of feathers. Country and weddings supplied.

BRICK LANE.

Abrahams, J., 56; Family grocer and provision dealer and general draper. Established 1875.

Adler, A. & Son, 6, Spital Street; Wholesale and retail Hebrew & English booksellers & silk "talaisim" manufacturers.

Alexander, 11, Osborn Street; Hairdresser and perfumer and chiropodist. Established 1886.

Bender, J., 4; Wholesale and retail leather and grindery dealer.

Cohen, Maurice, 93, Hanbury Street; Hairdresser perfumer, and dentist.

Crosky, Jos., 82, Old Montague Street; Tailors' trimmings and drapery shop.

Feldman, J. & Co., 2, Osborn St.; Exchange, banking, passage and commission agents. Est. 1886.

LONDON.
Commercial Directory of the Jews of Gt. Britain.

Freud, S., 7, Old Montague Street; Wholesale Manchester and general merchant in drapery, job and fancy goods. Also foreign goose feathers.

Herson Jos., 32, Hanbury St. (also at 15, Wilkes St.); Wholesale & retail grocer & provision merchant. Dealer in oil, Dutch & Scotch herrings & dried fruit.

Israel, B., 147; Wholesale and export cabinet maker, upholsterer, looking-glass and picture-frame manufacturer. Established 1881.

Joseph, Barnet, 62, Great Garden Street; dealer in and manufacturer of furniture, and upholsterer to the trade.

Korobinski, S., 111, Hanbury Street; Family grocer and provision dealer.

Leberman, M., 24, Great Garden Street; Montague deposit and loan office.

Levy, A., 70; London and Leeds Matzo Co., cakes and confectionery. Country orders received. Bakery: Chicksand Street.

Levy, Mark, 144, Wentworth Street, English and foreign fruiterer. Established 1864.

Mallimson, J., 48, Hanbury Street; Wholesale and retail Hebrew and English bookseller and dealer in silk "talaisim." All kinds of Am. novels and newspapers.

Marco, M., 35; Gasfitter, plumber, drain-worker, &c.

Pearl, E., 20; Plain and fancy cap-peak manufacturer. Established 1883.

Rosenberg, M., 14, Osborn Street; East London baths Under ecclesiastical authority.

Rubenstein, J., 14, Great Garden Street; Contracting carpenter and builder. City and country orders.

Spiro, H. & Co., 12; Tobacconist and foreign and domestic cigars & cigarette manufacturer.

LONDON.

Commercial Directory of the Jews of Gt. Britain.

Tax, Samuel, 138; Hairdresser, perfumer and chiropodist, tobacconist and cigarette manufacturer. Established 1875.

Walter, L. & P. & Son, Fournier Street; Wholesale clothiers.

Weinberg, J. 77; Hairdresser, chiropodist and dentist, also watchmaker. Established 1872.

Wolbrown, R., 58; Woollen and Manchester Job Co. and tailors' trimmings.

Zelinski, Leon, 19, Osborn St.; Wholesale Manchester and general merchant in drapery, job and fancy goods.

COMMERCIAL STREET.

Angel, Coleman, 130; Importer of washable gilt and coloured mouldings aud patent silvered sheet, and lithographers.

Barnett, G., 85; Wholesale and export boot and shoe manufacturer. Est. 1850.

Brezinsky, H. & Co., 50, Wentworth Street; Wholesale baby-linen manufacturers and warehousemen.

Greenfield, W., 71; Wholesale and export cocoa, chocolate, and French Nougat manufacturer.

Ludski, B. & Son, 63; Manufacturer of surgical instruments. Est. 1873.

Miller, L., 222; Wholesale & retail clothier, juvenile outfitter and waterproofer.

Silverstone, P. and Son, 149; Tailors, hosiers, and outfitters, cutters, and makers for the trade. Work done on the premises. Also at Upper St., Islington.

Shreider, L. & T., 57; Wholesele manufacturing furriers.

LONDON.

Commercial Directory of the Jews of Gt. Britain.

WHITE'S ROW.

Lyons, Leonard, 1–2; Wholesale and retail oilman. Passover oils and groceries supplied. Est 1878.

(SHAFTESBURY AVENUE.)

Marks, A., 163; House-furnisher and upholsterer. Est. 1883.

(SOHO.)

Morris, H., 42, Gerard Street; Master and custom tailor.

SPITAL SQUARE, E.C.

Davis, Joseph, 22; Manufacturer of men's and ladies' clothing.

Jacobs, W. Wholesale clothier.

Moss Brothers. Woollen merchants.

STONEY LANE, E.C.

Cohen, S., 6a; Boot maker.

Defries, D., 56; Gasfitter and Plumber.

Deyong, S., 9; Wholesale clothier.

Farbstein, J., 8; Hairdresser.

Goldenfelt, A., 7; Hosier.

Levy, J., 4; Merchant tailor.

Pollock, 4a; Tobacconist.

Silver, H. and E., 10a; Caterers, cooks and confectioners.

Singer, S., 10; Auctioneer.

LONDON.

Commercial Directory of the Jews of Gt. Britain.

STRATFORD.

Blumel, A., 10, Angel Lane; Watchmaker & jeweller. Work done for the trade. Speciality in musical boxes and mechanical figures.

Freedman, M., 198, The Grove, and 453, New Cross Road, S.E., and 65, Barking Road, E.; Furniture dealer.

TEMPLE.

Montefiore, J., (middle); Barrister.

Montefiore, J., (cloister's); Barrister.

THEOBALD'S ROAD, W.C.

Blackstone, Benj., 51; Master tailor. Est. 1878.

THROGMORTON AVENUE, E.C.

Marks, A. S., 30; Stockjobber.

Mocatta & Goldsmith, 7; Bullion brokers.

Montefiore, L. J., 10; Stockbroker.

Raphael, R. & Sons, 25; Merchants.

UPPER RUSSELL STREET.

Samuel & Rosenfeld, 3; Skin merchants.

WALWORTH ROAD, S.E.

Cohen, A. J., 115; Water proofer and clothier.

Gabriel, J., 324; Tobacco manufacturer.

Golding, M., 109a; Watch and clock maker, jeweller and optician.

Levine, H. and Co., 200; Butchers.

LONDON.

Commercial Directory of the Jews of Gt. Britain.

Levy, A., 51 ; Merchant tailor.
Levy, Mrs. R., 399 ; Fruiterer.
Lyons, A., Jun., 57 ; House-furnisher.

WANDSWORTH.

Dangowitz, M., 563 York Road ; Branch, 33, Oldridge Road, Balham ; Window glass & paper-hangings.
Nieman, Isaac, 455, York Road ; High-class custom tailor and tailor for the trade.

WARDOUR STREET, W.

Blackstone, J., 164 ; Master and custom tailor. Est. 1867.
Fersht, B. A., 151 ; Diamond mounter and jeweller.
Fersht, S., 151 ; Master and custom tailor.
Harris, Chas., 76 ; Pastrycook, confectioner and fancy baker. Under ecclesiastical authority.

WARWICK STREET, REGENT STREET.

Morris, J., 52 ; Master tailor. Est. 1880.

WENTWORTH STREET, E.C.

Abrahams, A., 19 ; Grocer, etc.
Ambus, A., 28 ; Draper.
Boam, J., 118 ; General dealer.
Boat, M., 17 ; Grocer.
Bonn, J., 2, Confectioner.
Boxer, P. ; Produce.
Cohen, D. and Son, 10 ; Grocers.

LONDON.

Commercial Directory of the Jews of Gt. Britain.

Cohen, L., 126 ; Oils.
Cohen, S., 20 ; Baker.
Davis, M., 133 ; Produce.
Freedman, A., 27a ; Clothier.
Frost, N., 143 ; Flour.
Geduld, N., 1 ; Butcher.
Landau, S., 137 ; Baker.
Levy, J., 135 ; Furnisher.
Levy, M., 144 ; Fruiterer.
Linda, D., 27 ; Butcher.
Lyons, S., 22 ; Confectioner.
Michaels, L., 116 ; Butcher.
Matthews, M., 131 ; Clothier.
Palkowski, L., 29 ; Chinaware.
Ruda, H., 139 ; Butcher.
Schweitzer, P., 134 ; Draper.
Silverstone, Mrs., 136 ; Butcher.
Specterman, M., 1 ; Butcher.
Solomons, 21 ; Boots and shoes.

WESTBOURNE GROVE, W.

Abrahams, 104 ; China and Glass Merchant.
Jacobs, 156 ; Lead Merchant.
Marks, Charles, 188 ; Fish merchant. Establ. 1878. Family orders punctually attended to.
Mendelson ; High-class photographer.
Middlevich, M., 232 ; Watchmaker, jeweller, optician, and engraver. Umbrella and stick manufacturer.

LONDON.

Commercial Directory of the Jews of Gt. Britain.

Oppenheim, J. and S. ; 66 ; Cigar merchants. And at 5, Porchester Road.

Phillips, N., 87 ; Furrier. And at 7, Ludgate Circus.

Rosenberg, M., 229 ; Builder and decorator.

Whitechapel Road, E.

Abrahamsohn, F. K., 29, Church Lane; Wholesale and retail manufacturer. Warsaw and Vienna wursht and sausages, smoked beef and tongues. Country orders for Passover received. Under ecclesiastical authority. Established 1888.

Alexander, Louis, 11, Osborn Street; Hairdresser, perfumer and chiropodist.

Bennett, Sydney, 64 ; Hosier and outfitter.

Brook, E., 31 ; wholesale and retail furrier.

Carlish, C., 66 ; Merchant tailor.

Cohen and Son, 10, Church Lane; Wholesale and retail woollen merchants and tailors.

Cohen, J., 47 ; English and foreign fancy dealer.

Cohen, M. and Co., Brady Street ; Grocer, etc.

Cohn, Bernhard, 249 ; Tailor and outfitter.

Cohnreich Bros., 79a ; Wholesale and retail boots and shoes. And at 28, Lower Marsh, Lambeth, and 198, Jamaica Road, S.E.

Crosky, Jos., 82, Old Montague Street ; Tailors' trimmings.

Davis, J., 62, High Street; House-furnisher.

Feinmesser, 23 ; Watchmaker.

LONDON.
Commercial Directory of the Jews of Gt. Britain.

Feldman, J. and Co., 2, Osborn Street; Exchange, banking, passage, and commission agents. Established 1886.

Franklin S., 1; Boot-and shoe dealer.

Freud, S., 7, Old Montague Street; General merchant.

Glanz, Isaac, 129, New Road; Retail hosier.

Gold, J. and A. and Co., 242; Wholesale and export "French Nougat" and fancy chocolate manufrs. Established 1883.

Goldberg, H., 123, New Road; Wholesale and export boot and shoe manufacturer. Established 1885.

Goldberg, Ph., 125, New Road; Wholesale and retail leather and grindery merchant. Est. 1884.

Goldstein, M., 26; House-furnisher.

Goorvitch, P., 30, Church Lane; Cigarette manufacturer, tobacconist and cigar importer.

Haimson, H. S., 21; Passage agents.

Harris, E., 15; Merchant tailor.

Joseph, A., 75; Merchant tailor.

Kattenberg, H. & Co., 36; Drapers.

Keyman & Gerhold, 243; Frame makers and upholsterers to the trade. Private orders received.

Koopman, E. H., 223; Picture-frame maker.

Leberman, M., 24, Gt. Garden Street; Financial agent.

Lewinstein, K., 60; General Printer.

Meczyk, P. and Co., 11, Church Lane; Exchange, banking, passage, and commission agents.

Michaels, Morris, 1, Charlotte Street; Wholesale and retail tailors' trimmings and drapers. Est. 1863.

Mordecai, A., 230; Cigar manufacturer.

LONDON.

Commercial Directory of the Jews of Gt. Britain.

Oldschool, Samuel, 255; Leather dealer and upper manufacturer.

Poliakoff, M., 252; High-class tailor and outfitter.

Rakusin, A. B., 31; Enamel ware.

Rosenbaum, J. R. and Co., 30; Milliners, fancy drapers and bridal outfitters.

Rosenberg, Moses, M., 14, Fieldgate Street; Odessa family baker. Grocers supplied.

Sakovitz, Louis, 204; Perforater to the boot trade.

Salmon and Gluckstein, 34; Cigar and Tobacco merchants.

Seelig, S., 73, New Road; Family butcher, poulterer, smoked and salt beef, etc. Established 1873.

Segal, A. & Co., 24, Church Lane; Wholesale general warehousemen. Silks, stuffs, velvets, prints, whites, etc. Established 1885.

Singer, R., 271; Watchmaker and jeweller.

Sobell, Lazarus, 60, Bakers' Row; Wholesale and retail mantle manufacturer. Ladies' own materials made up. A large stock always on hand. Established 1888.

Solomon, M., 127, New Road; Rubber stamp manufacturer, and agent for life insurance, accidents, fire, burglary, plate-glass, building societies, etc. Established 1882.

Warschawsky, M. and Son, 8, "The Mount"; High-class tailors.

Weber, I. and Sons, 218; Cigar manufacturers.

Zelinski, Leon, 19, Osborn Street; Wholesale Manchester and job and fancy goods merchant.

Zuckerman, S., 8, Church Lane; General cabinet manufacturer and house furnisher.

LONDON.

Court Directory of the Jews of Gt. Britain.

Adler, Rev. Hermann, Ph.D., M.A., Chief Rabbi, 22, Finsbury Square, and 5, Queensboro' Terrace, Bayswater, W.

Adler, Markus Nathan, M.A., 22, Craven Hill, Hyde Park, W.

Abrahams, Israel, M.A., 70, Bromdesbury Road, Kilburn, N.W.

Barnet, L., M.D., Broadshaw Gardens, North Hampstead.

Cohen, Abm , M.A., M.D., 67, Warrington Crescent.

Cohen, Abraham, M.A., M.D., 67, Warrington Crescent, W.

Cohen, Abraham S., 4, Portman Mansions, Marylebone Road, W.

Cohen, Alfred, 80, Leabroke Grove Road, W.

Cohen, Alfred, 75, Queen's Crescent, Haverstock Hill, N.W.

Cohen, Alfred D., 24, St. George's Square, N.W.

Cohen, Alfred L., 106, Westbourne Terrace, W.

Cohen, Arthur, Q.C., 6, Holland Park, W.

Cohen, Arthur, 359, Holloway Road, N.

Cohen, Barnett, 23, Gordon Square, W.C.

Cohen, Barron J., 29, Compton Terrace, Up. St., N.

LONDON.

Court Directory of the Jews of Gt. Britain.

Cohen, Barry, 72, London Wall, E.C., and Berea, Wood Church Road, W. Hampstead, N.W.

Cohen, Benj. Louis, M.P., 30, Hyde Park Gardens, W. Carlton, Junior Carlton, Conservative and City Carlton Clubs.

Cohen, D., 4, Portman Mansions, Marylebone Road.

Cohen, David de Lara, 2, Portman Mansions, Marylebone Road.

Cohen, Edward Israel, 37, Bedford Square, W.C.

Cohen, Emanuel, 2, Museum Chambers, Bury Street.

Cohen, Lionel B. 44, Sussex Gardens.

Cohen, Rev. Isaac, Great St. Helens.

Dyte, David Hyman, Physician, 12, Derby street.

Franklin Arthur E., 29, Pembridge gardens.

Franklin, Chas., 57, Gibson square, Islington.

Franklin, Ellis A., 25, Porchester terrace.

Franklin, Ernest L., 9, Pembridge gardens.

Franklin, Samuel, 1, Raymond buildings, W.C., and Clarememont road, Surbiton.

Friedlander, M., Ph.D., Tavistock House, Tavistock Villas, Tavistock Square.

Friedlander, Rev. Joseph, Sec. Chief R., 17, Elgin Avenue, W.

LONDON.

Court Directory of the Jews of Gt. Britain.

Gaster, Rev. Dr. M., Chief R. Sp. and Port., 34, Warwick Road, Maida Hill, W.

Gollancz, Rev. Herman, M.A., 39, Clifton Gardens.

Gollancz, Rev. Saml. M., 154, Houndsditch.

Goldsmid, Capt. Lionel Campbell, 31, Manilla Gardens, North Kensington, W.

Goldsmid, George, 114, Piccadiily, W.

Goldsmid, Lady Louisa, 13, Portman Square, W., and Western House, Bishop's down, Tunbridge Wells.

Goldsmid, Miss F., 49-55, Brook Street, W.

Goldsmid, Misses, 20, Portman Square, W., and Tongswood, Hawkhurst.

Goldsmid, Mrs., 45, Bayswater Square, W.

Goldsmid, Mrs. Alfred, 45, Ennismore Gardens.

Goldsmid, Sir Julian, Bart., M.P., F.R.G.S., M.R.S.L., D.L., J.P., 105, Piccadilly, W.; Liberal Clubs, S.W. and Somerhill Brooks, Reform, Devonshire and National, Tonbridge, Kent.

Goldsmidt, Walter, 16, The Grove, Bolton, S.W.

Gompertz. Major, B. T. M., 101, Landsdowne Road.

Harris, Henry Saloman, 63, Coleman street, and 53, Priory road, Kilburn, N.W.

LONDON.

Court Directory of the Jews of Gt. Britain.

Harris, Henry, 6, Paul's crescent, Camden square.

Harris, Joseph, 20, Dawson place, Bayswater, W., & Lower Coombe, Bovey Tracy, Devon.

Harris, Joseph, Shobrooke house, Willow bridge road, N.

Harris, Nathaniel, 2, Russell square.

Harris, Rev. Isidor, M.A., 192, Portsdown road, W.

Harris, Rev. Joseph, M.A., 7, Randolph gardens.

Harris, Rev. Raphael, M.A., 77, Sutherland avenue.

Hart, Alderman E., 14, Moorgate street,

Hart, Alfred J., 23, Moorgate street, 4, Beech croft, Bickley, Kent.

Hart, Edward, 38, Bedford square.

Hart, Edward L, 216, Piccadilly.

Hart, Edwin, 33, Bedford Row, and 15, Winchester Road, South Hampstead.

Hart, Ernest, 38, Wimpole Street; 429, Strand, and Fairlawn, Totteridge, Herts.

Hart, F. V., 10, Portman Mansions, Marylebone Road.

Hart, F. J., L.L.B., 7, Alpha Road, W.

Hart, George F., 12, Old Square, Lincoln's Inn, and Harley Lodge, Mare's Field Gardens, Hampstead, N.W.

LONDON.

Court Directory of the Jews of Gt. Britain.

Hart, H. L., L.L.B., Goldsmith Buildings, Temple, and the Pines, Putney Hill.

Hart, J. M., F.R.G.S., K.G.M., 20, Pembridge Square, W.

Hart, Lady, 38, Cadogan place, S.W.

Hast, Rev., Marcus, 21, Gt. Prescott Street.

Herschill, Geo., M.D., 5, West street, Finsbury.

Isaacs, Sir H. A., Kt. and ex-Lord Mayor.

Kisch, Albert, 186, Sutherland avenue, W.

Kisch, Augustus, 148, Aldersgate street, and 6, Brondesbury road, Kilburn, N.W.

Kisch, Benj., 148, Brick court, Temple, E.C.

Kisch, Henry Joseph, 27, Marlborough place, St. John's Wood, N.W.

Leon, Herbert Samuel, M.P., 98, Mount Street, W.; Devonshire Club, S.W., and Bletchley Park, Bletchley.

Lerner, Rev. Dr., Chief of Federation of Synagogues, 46, Gt. Prescott Street.

Lipman, Rev. N., Chief of Shochetim, 61, Mansell Street, E.C.

Lowy, Rev. A., 100, Sutherland Avenue.

Magnus, Sir Philip, knt, 48, Gloucester Place, Portman Square, W.

LONDON.

Court Directory of the Jews of Gt. Britain.

Marks, J. M., 32, Russell Square.

Marks, Rev. David Woolf, 30, Dorset Square, N.W.

Montagu, Charles, 3, Colville Square.

Montagu, Hyman, F.S.A., 34, Queen's Gardens, Bayswater, W.

Montagu, Sam., M.P., 12, Kensington Palace Gardens and South Stoneham House, Southampton, Hampshire.

Montagu, Samuel Alfred, 3, Palestine Place, Cambridge Road, E.

Montague, Sydney John, 7, Kensington Gardens Square, Bayswater, W.

Montefiore, Lieut. Col. Emanuel, 7, Lancaster St., Hyde Park, W.

Montefiore, Sir Francis A., Bart. 42, Upper Grosvenor Street, W., and Worth Park, Crawley, Sussex.

Montefiore, Arthur Sebag, 2, Palace Houses, Kensington Gardens, W.

Montefiore, Claud Goldsmid, 12, Portland Square, W., and Coldeast, Southampton.

Montefiore, Edmund Sebag, 9, Oxford Square, W.

Montefiore, Jacob, 35, Hyde Park Square, W.

Montefiore, John, 6, Middle Temple Lane, E.C.

LONDON.

Court Directory of the Jews of Gt. Britain.

Montefiore, Jos. B., 36, Kensington Gardens Sq., W.

Montefiore, Jos. Gompertz, 14, Westbourne Park Road, W.

Montefiore, Jos. Sebag, 4, Hyde Park Gardens, W., and East Cliff Lodge, St. Laurence, Ramsgate.

Montefiore, Leslie, 41, Warwick Road, Maida Vale.

Montefiore, Mrs, 4, Great Stanhope Street, W., and Worth Park, Crawley, Sussex.

Montefiore, Mrs. Goldsmid, 18, Portman Sq., W.

Moss, H.D., 73, Queensboro terrace, W.

Moss, J., 53, Acacia road, W.

Moss, J., 33, Bassett road, W.

Moss, J., 76, Kensington gardens, W.

Moss, N., 73, Lodbroke grove road.

Moss, Ralph, 123, Sutherland avenue.

Moss, Richard, 60, Warwick street, Pumlico.

Moss, Sam, 31, Athelstan road, Boro' E.

Moss, Sam., 158, Lancaster road, W.

Moss, Saul, 19, Bassier road.

Myers, Asher Isaac, 2, Finsbury Square, E.C.

Phillips, J., M.A., M.D., F.R.C. of Physicians, 71, Grosvenor street, W.

LONDON.

Court Directory of the Jews of Gt. Britain.

Phillips, Sidney, M.D., 62, Upper Berkley street, W.

Raphael, Herbert Henry, 4, Cumberland place, Regent's park, N.W., and Rose Ct., Havering-atte-bower, Essex.

Rosenberg, Isaac, 45, Bassett Road, W.

Rosenberg, John Joseph, 11, Tredegar Square. E.

Rosenberg, Julius, 32, Tredegar Square, E.

Rosenberg, Miss, 27, Albany Street, N.W.

Rosenberg, Mrs., 30, Chalcourt Crescent, Regent's Park, N.W.

Rosenberg, Mrs., 35, Clifton Gardens, W.

Rosenfeld, Abm., 118, Highbury New Park, N.

Rosenfeld, Benedict, 92, Highbury New Park, N.

Rosenfeld, Isaac, 2; Cleveland Gardens, W.

Rosenstein, Jacob, 8, Highbury Quadrant, N.

Rosentreid, Nathaniel, 44, Cambridge Gardens, W.

Rosenthal, Alfred Ephraim, F.R.G.S., 1, Furnival's Inn, E.C.

Rosenthal, Julius Loewe, 21, Southampton St., W.

Rosenthal, Lewis Arthur, 24, Kelvin Road, Highbury, N.

Rosenthal, Lionel Henry, 12, Lyric Chambers, Whitcomb Street, W.E.

LONDON.

Court Directory of the Jews of Gt. Britain.

Rothschild, Lord, 148, Piccadilly, W.; New Court, St. Swithin's Lane; Book's, Marlborough.

Rothschild, Dowager Lady de, 19, Grosvenor Place, S.W., and Aston Clinton, Bucks.

Rothschild, Baron Alfred Chas. de, St. Swithin's Lane; Seymour Place, Mayfair, and Halton, Tring, W.

Rothschild, Baron Ferdinand James de, M.P., 143, Piccadilly, W.; Waddesdon Manor, Aylesbury, and Manor House, Upper Winchenden, Bucks.

Rothschild. David, 13, Roland Gardens, S.W.

Rothschild, Alfred August, 37, Cleveland Square.

Rothschild, Leopold de, 5, Hamilton Place, Piccadilly, W., St. Swithin's Lane; Ascott, Leighton Buzzard, and Palace House, Newmarket.

Rothschild, Miss Alice, 142, Piccadilly, W.

Rothschild, Theodore, 22, Jermyn Street, S.W.

Samuel, Sir Saul, K.C.M.G., C.B. and Lady, 15, Courtfield Gardens, S. Kensington, S.W., and 9, Victoria Street, S.W.

Samuel, Rev. Isaac, 74, Sutherland Avenue, W.

Samuel, Isaac B., 1, Hanover Terrace, Regent's Park, N.W., and Westbourne House, Surbiton.

Samuel, Henry Silvester, 80, Onslow Gardens, S.W.

LONDON.

Court Directory of the Jews of Gt. Britain.

Samuel, Alderman Marcus, 20, Portland Place, W.

Sassoon, Sir Albert, Bart., C.S.I., 25, Kensington Grove, S.W., 1, Eastern terrace, Brighton. Sans Souci, Bombay, and Garden Reach, Poonah.

Sassoon, Arthur, 8, Pembroke studios, Pembroke gardens, W.

Sassoon, David, 8, Albert gate, S.W. 8, King's gardens, West Brighton. Tulchan lodge, Elginshire.

Sassoon, Edward, 25, Kensington grove, and 1, Eastern terrace, Brighton.

Sassoon, Frederic, 125, Piccadilly, W.

Sassoon, Reuben David, 1, Belgrave square, W., and 7, Queen's gardens, West Brighton.

Schloss, Albert, 21, North Audley Street.

Schloss, Daniel, 120, Westbourne Terrace.

Schloss, D. F., Knaresboro' Place, Cromwell Road.

Schloss, Joseph, 113, King Henry's Road, N.W.

Schloss, Leopold, 17, Leinston Gardens, W.

Schloss, L. R., 87, Gloucester Terrace.

Schloss, S., 30, Leinston Gardens, W.

Simmons, S. M., L.L.B., B.A., 49, Finsbury pavement.

Simon, Sir John, K.C.B., F.R.S., D.C.L., L.L.D., 10, Kensington square.

LONDON.

Court Directory of the Jews of Gt. Britain.

Singer, Rev. Simeon, 52, Levister Square, W.

Spiers, Rev. B., Doyen Ecclesiastical Court, 20, Christopher Street, Finsbury Square.

Spyer, E. S. and S., 6, Union Street, Old Broad Street; 35, New Broad Street; 225, Finchley Road; and Homefield, Netherall Gardens, S. Hampstead.

Stern, Sydney James, M.P., 10, Gt. Stanhope Street, Mayfair, W.; Devonshire, Reform, St. James', and Bachelors' Clubs; and Hengreave Hall, Bury St. Elginaw, W.

Waley, Alfred, 6, Hyde Park Square, W.

Waley, J. F., 9, Old Square, W.C.

Waley, Montefiore Simon, 14, Dawson Place, Bayswater, W.

Waley, Mrs., 22, Devonshire Place, Portland Place.

Wolf, Lucien; Historian.

Worms, Baron de, F.R.G.S., F.S.A., M.R.S.L., F.G.S., L.D., J.P., 17, Park Crescent, Portland Place, W.; Milton Park, Egham, Surrey; and 27, Adelaide Crescent, Brighton.

Worms, Rt. Hon. Baron Henry de, M.P., F.R.S., 42, Grosvenor Place; Carlton, Junior Carlton, Constitutional, City of London Clubs; and Henley Park, Guildford.

LONDON.

Court Directory of the Jews of Gt. Britain.

PERIODICAL PUBLICATIONS.

Jewish Chronicle, 2, Finsbury Square, E.C.

Jewish World, 8, South Street, Finsbury.

" Palestina," Chovevei Zion Quarterly, 11, Bevis Marks, E.C.

Sulamith, 82, Brick Lane, Spitalfields.

LONDON.

Synagogal Directory of the Jews of Gt. Britain.

ECCLESIASTICAL COURT.

CHIEF RABBI:
REV. DR. HERMAN ADLER.

Rev. BERNARD SPIERS, DAYAN, 20, Christopher St., Finsbury.

Rev. SUSMAN COHEN, DAYAN.

Rev. N. LIPMAN, Chief of Shochetim, 61, Mansell Street.

Rev. Dr. LERNER, Chief Magid of Federation of Synagogues.

Rev. Dr. MOSES GASTER, Chief Rabbi of the Spanish and Portuguese Congregations of the British Empire.

ANGLO-JEWISH ASSOCIATION.

Sir Julian Goldsmid, Bart., M.P., President.
Vice-Presidents :—The Right Hon. Lord Rothschild; Sir Henry A. Isaacs, Kt.; Ellis A. Franklin, Esq.; Alf. G. Henriques, Esq.; F. D. Mocatta, Esq.; Sir Albert Sassoon, Bart., C.S.I.; Reuben D. Sassoon, Esq.; Leopold Schloss, Esq.; Sir John Simon.
Treasurer: Ellis A. Franklin, Esq.   M. Duparc, Secretary.

BOARD OF DEPUTIES.

LONDON SYNAGOGUES.

SPANISH AND PORTUGUESE: Manuel Castello, Joshua M. Levy, (Auditor) G. Lindo, C.C., A. Mocatta, and J. Sebag Montefiore, J.P., (Vice-President), Esqs.
GREAT: L. De Rothschild, D. Marks, and M. Hart, Esqs.
CENTRAL: D. L. Alexander, B.A., F. Davis, J. Jones, Esqs.
HAMBRO': S. Jacobs, and A. Salomon, Esqs.
HAMPSTEAD:
NEW: L. Ososki and S. Woolf, Esqs.
BAYSWATER: B. L. Cohen, L.C.C., and S. Heilbut, Esqs.

LONDON.

Synagogal Directory of the Jews of Gt. Britain.

WESTERN: S. V. Abrahams, Esq.
MAIDEN LANE: Henry Harris, Esq.
BOROUGH (NEW): J. A. Cohen, Esq.
NORTH LONDON: B. Birnbaum, Esq.
DALSTON: S. Simon, Esq.
EAST LONDON: A. Levy, and L. Levy, Esqs.
NEW WEST END: E. A. Franklin, and A. Cohen, Q.C., (President), Esqs.
JOHN'S WOOD: Salomon Spyer, Esq., C.C.
SPITAL SQUARE: S. Montagu, Esq., M.P.

PROVINCIAL SYNAGOGUES.

BELFAST: No election.
BIRMINGHAM: Henry Nathan, Esq.
BOSTON, LINCOLN: No election.
BRIGHTON: Lewis Lewis, Esq.
CANTERBURY: T. Lumley, Esq.
CHATHAM: A. B. Salmon, Esq.
CORK: No election.
DOVER: A. Tuck, Esq.
DUBLIN: John D. Rosenthal, Esq., L.L.D.
DUNDEE: No election.
HULL: Barnett Barnett, Esq.
LEEDS: Too late for election.
LIVERPOOL (OLD): Benjamin Newgass, Esq.
MANCHESTER (OLD): Hon. Walter Rothschild.
MANCHESTER (SOUTH): J. Tobias, Esq.
MERTHYR TYDVIL: Z. Goodman, Esq.
MIDDLESBORO': Arthur Cohen, Esq.
NEWCASTLE-ON-TYNE: H. S. Mendelssohn, Esq.
NEWPORT (MONMOUTH): L. Schloss, Esq.
NORWICH: H. H. Haldenstein, Esq., B.A.
NOTTINGHAM: A. E. Franklin, Esq.
SHEFFIELD: Lt. Col· Goldsmid, D.A.A.G.
SOUTHAMPTON: L. Davis, Esq.
SOUTHPORT: No election.
STOCKPORT: No election.
STOCKTON: Lucien Wolf, Esq.
SUNDERLAND: O. J. Simon, Esq.
SWANSEA: Dr. L. Barnet.
CHELTENHAM: A. A. Jones, Esq.

Solicitor and Secretary: Lewis Emanuel, Esq., 36, Finsbury. Circus, London, E.C.   *Bankers*: Messrs. S. Montagu & Co.

LONDON.

Synagogal Directory of the Jews of Gt. Britain.

COUNCIL OF THE UNITED SYNAGOGUE.

Hyman A. Abrahams, Esq.
Samuel Abrahams, Esq.
S. Alexander, Esq.
A. Arnholz, Esq.
Ephraim Barnett, Esq.
Henry Barnett, Esq.
A. H. Beddington, Esq.
Henry E. Beddington, Esq.
Hyam E. Beddington, Esq.
Maurice Beddington, Esq.
David Benjamin, Esq.
Moss Benjamin, Esq.
M. Benjamin, Esq.
Ellis Berg, Esq.
J. Berg, Esq.
J. Bergtheil, Esq.
B. Binbaum, Esq.
R. Z. Bloomfield, Esq.
A. Brodziak, Esq.
J. Chapman, Esq.
Benjamin L. Cohen, Esq.
J. A. Cohen, Esq.
Leonard Cohen, Esq.
Moss Cohen, Esq.
Cæsar Cohen, Esq.
Louis Davidson, Esq.
D. Davis, Esq.
David Davis, Esq.
Frederick Davis, Esq.
Noah Davis, Esq.
Lawrence Engel, Esq.
L. Farmer, Esq.
S. Finberg, Esq.
J. Flatau, Esq,
A. S. Fleisig, Esq.
E. N. Frankenstein, Esq.
Albert Friedlander, Esq.
John Goldhill, Esq.
E. Graumann, Esq.
J. Grunbaum, Esq.

F. M. Halford, Esq.
J. M Harris, Esq.
H. M. Harris, Esq.
Henry Harris, Esq.
Henry Hart, Esq.
Maurice Hart, Esq.
Lawrence Hyam, Esq.
Saul Isaac, Esq.
Asher Isaacs, Esq.
Sir H. A. Isaacs, Kt. & Ald.
Joseph M. Isaacs, Esq.
D. L. Jacobs, Esq.
John Jacobs, Esq.
S. Jacobs, Esq.
Albert H. Jessel, Esq.
Nathan S. Joseph, Esq.
Coleman Jones, Esq.
Ashur Keysor, Esq.
M. Kruszinki, Esq.
E. Lawton, Esq.
Simeon Lazarus, Esq.
A. Leon, Esq.
Alexander Levy, Esq.
H. Levy, Esq.
Lewis Levy, Esq.
A. J. Lion, Esq.
Lion Lion, Esq.
Edward Lucas, Esq.
Henry Lucas, Esq.
H. Lutto, Esq.
Lewis Lyons, Esq.
Joseph Magnus, Esq.
L. Marchant, Esq.
I. M. Marks, Esq.
Herbert P. Marsden, Esq.
Herman Meyer, Esq.
P. Ornstein, Esq., *Secy.*
Samuel Montagu, Esq., M.P.
Assur H. Moses, Esq.
S. Moses, Esq., M.A.

LONDON.

Synagogal Directory of the Jews of Gt. Britain.

Samuel E. Moss, Esq.
S. Mossel, Esq.
Asher I. Myers, Esq.
Wolf Myers, Esq.
Henry Nathan, Esq.
L. E. Nathan, Esq.
Louis Ososki, Esq.
Geo. Faudel Phillips, Esq.
S. J. Phillips, Esq.
A. Rosenfeld, Esq.
Leopold De Rothschild, Esq.
Rt. Hon. Lord Rothschild.
M. A. Rozelaar, Esq.
Charles Samuel, Esq.
Stuart M. Samuel, Esq.
Solomon Schloss, Esq.
J. Schwarzchild, Esq.
J. L. Simmonds, Esq.

Henry Simmons, Esq.
Simon Simons, Esq.
Henry Solomon, Esq.
Saul Solomons Esq.
H. J. Solomons, Esq.
I. Spielman, Esq.
A. E. Sydney, Esq.
Adolph Tuck, Esq.
S. Vander Linde, Esq.
B. L. Van Praagh, Esq.
B. Van Staveren, Esq.
Isaac Weber, Esq.
Simon Wharman, Esq.
Albert Woolf, Esq.
Saul Woolf, Esq.
The Right Hon. Baron H. de Worms, M.P.

GREAT SYNAGOGUE, James' Place, Aldgate.

Wardens: T.R.H. Lord Rothschild, and A. Rosenfeld, Esq.

Representatives: Isaiah M. Marks, Esq., *Finance Member;* Messrs. M. Benjamin, A. L. Friedlander, H. Meyer, B. Van Staveren, I. Weber, and S. Wharman.

Local Committee: Messrs. M. Benjamin, Ralph Lazarus, Hon. Walter Lionel Rothschild, L. Simmons, I. Weber and S. Wharman. Revs. M. Hast and A. E. Gordon, *Readers.* Alfred Henry, Esq., *Sec.* Mr. S. Levy, *Beadle and Collector.*

NEW SYNAGOGUE, Gt. Helen's, Bishopsgate.

Wardens: Messrs. Louis Ososki and Saul Woolf.

Representatives: Mr. Ephraim Barnett, *Finance Member*; Messrs. B. Barnett, Coleman Defries, H. Lutto, H. Lyons, and S. Moses, M.A.

Local Committee: Messrs. H. Barnett, H. Lyons, S. Moses, M.A., S. F. Feldman, A. M. Wartski, B. Coster, L. Reed, B. Woolf, Henry Rosenbaum, and G. Tack.

Rev. M. A. Epstein, *Reader*, Rev. I. Cohen, *Secretary.* Samson, *Beadle and Collector*, 136, Houndsditch.

LONDON.

Synagogal Directory of the Jews of Gt. Britain.

HAMBRO' SYNAGOGUE, Fenchurch Street.

Wardens: Messrs. S. Jacobs and B. L. Van Praagh.

Representatives: Mr. S. Vander Linde, *Finance Member*, and L. Marchant.

Local Committee: Messrs. L. Harris, G. A. Isaacs, L. Marchant, M. Rosenberg, S. Rosenberg. L. J. Salomons & Abraham Solomons. Dr. Gollancz, *Reader.* J. Salomons, Esq., *Secretary, 13, Spital Square, Bishopsgate, E.*

CENTRAL SYNAGOGUE, Great Portland Street.

Wardens: Samuel E. Moss and Leonard L. Cohen.

Representatives: Mr. H. Simmons, *Finance Member;* Messrs. Alfred H. Beddington, F. Davis, A. Isaacs, S. J. Phillips, and Leopold de Rothschild.

Local Committee: Messrs. S. Trenner, Dr. M. Friedlander, Leopold de Rothschild, A. H. Beddington, A. Isaacs, S. J. Phillips, and F. Davis. Rev. David Fay, *Minister.* Mr. P. Vallentine, *Beadle and Collector.*

BAYSWATER SYNAGOGUE, Chichester Place, Harrow Road.

Wardens: Messrs. S. Lazarus and E. Lucas.

Representatives: Mr. L. E. Nathan, *Finance Member;* Messrs. J. Bergtheil, A. Brodziak Louis Davidson, J. Flatau, A. H. Jessel and Wolf Myers.

Local Committee: Messrs. J. Bergtheil, David Benjamin, A. Brodziak, B. L. Cohen, J. Flatau, S. Heilbut, I. A. Joseph, H. Lucas, Wolf Myers and C. Samuel. Rev. Dr. H. Gollancz, *Minister.* Rev. I. Samuel, *Reader.* Rev. R. Harris, *Sec., 77, Sutherland Gardens, W.* Mr. L. Cohen, *Beadle and Collector.*

BOROUGH SYNAGOGUE, Heygate Street, Walworth.

Wardens: Messrs. J. A. Cohen, and H. J. Solomons.

Representatives: Mr. D. Davies, *Finance Member;* Messrs. H. M. Harris and A. Leon.

Local Committee: Messrs. B. H. Abrahams, M. Benjamin, H. M. Harris, B. Jacobs, D. L. Jacobs, Jacob Joseph, A. Leon, R. J. Moses, A. H. Woolf and J. Woolf. F. L. Cohen, *Minister and Secretary.*

LONDON.

Synagogal Directory of the Jews of Gt. Britain.

EAST LONDON SYNAGOGUE, Stepney Green, E.
Wardens: Messrs. Lewis Levy and S. Finberg.
Representatives: Messrs. A. Pfeisig, *Finance Member;* M. Cohen, H. Harris, and E. Lawton.
Local Committee: Messrs. M. Cohen, M. Harris, E. Lawton, David Moses, E. Norden and E. J. Proops,
Rev. I. Greenberg, *Reader.*   J. F. Stern, *Minister & Sec.*
Mr. A. Winkel, *Beadle.*

JOHN'S WOOD SYNAGOGUE, Abbey Road.
Wardens: Messrs. Adolph Arnholz and Albert Woolf.
Representatives: Mr. A. I. Myers, *Finance Member.*
Messrs. R. Z. Bloomfield, L. Farmer, E. N. Frankenstein, A. Woolf.
Local Committee: Messrs. H. A. Abrahams, R. Z. Bloomfield, A. Davis, M. De Saxe. E. N. Frankenstein, M. A. Green, G. S. Marks, and R. Sonnenthal.
Rev. B. Berliner, *Minister.*   Rev. Mr. Price, *Sec. and Assistant Reader.*

NEW WEST-END SYNAGOGUE, Peter's Pl., Bayswater.
Warden: Messrs. Frederick M. Halford and Isidore Spielman.
Representative: J. Schwarzchild, *Finance Member;* J. Gruneberg, H. H. Marsden, H. Nathan and Stuart M. Samuel.
Local Committee: L. D. Cohen, S. S. Hyam, H. Landau, L. Mandelson, H. P. Marsden, Samuel Montagu, M.P., C. D. Moss, Henry Nathan and Dr. A. Wolff, Esq. Rev. S. Singer, *Minister.* Rev. M. Haines, *Sec., 34, Talbot Road, Wesbourne Park, W.*   Mr. Humphrey J. Phillips, *Beadle.*

NORTH LONDON SYNAGOGUE, John Street, Thornhill Road.
Wardens: Messrs. W. Flatau and A. Tuck.
Representatives: Mr. J. Goldhill, *Finance Member;* Messrs. S. Alexander and S. Mossel.
Local Committee: Messrs. S. Alexander, S. Birn, B. Daltroff, I. Davis, J. M. Lissack, Junr., J. Magnus, M. Spiegel and L. Themans, Rev. J. A. Goldstein, *Minister and Sec., 38, Milner Square, N.* Rev. Muns, *Reader.* Mr. Myers, *Beadle and Collector.*

LONDON.

Synagogal Directory of the Jews of Gt. Britain.

DALSTON SYNAGOGUE, Poet's Road.

Wardens: Messrs. M. Kruszinski and M. A. Rozelaar.
Representatives: Messrs. S. Simons, *Finance Member;* J. Berg, J. Chapman, C. Cohen, and Lion Lion.
Local Committee: Messrs. J. Bernstein, J. Birn, J. Chapman, C. Cohen, E. Gompers, S. Hess, L. Lazarus, P. Leuw, M. L. Lion and A. P. Levy Tebbitt. Rev. M. Hyamson, B.A., *Minister and Sec.* Rev. J. Lessor, *Reader.* J. J. Bruske, *Choir Master.*

SPANISH AND PORTUGUESE SYNAGOGUE, Bevis Marks.

Wardens: A. D. de Pass, E. Arbib, G. Lindo, E. H. d'Avigdor, Esqs. Edward Sassoon, Esq., *Treasurer.* E. H. Lindo, Esq., *Secretary, 11, Bevis Marks.* S. L. Cohen, *Assistant Secretary.* Rev. S. J. Roco, *Minister.*
BRANCH—Bryanston Street, W. The same Wardens. Rev. Joseph Piperno, *Minister.*

WESTERN SYNAGOGUE, Alban's Place, Haymarket.

S. V. Abrahams & M. Harris, Esqs., *Wardens.* E. Loewe, Esq., *Treasurer.* J. Sax, Esq., *Overseer.* Rev. H. Davids, *First Reader.* Rev. L. Canter, *Second Reader and Secretary.* M. Raphael, *Beadle and Collector.*

MAIDEN LANE SYNAGOGUE, Maiden-lane, Covent Garden.

H. Harris, Esq., *President.* H. S. Harris and J. S. Lyon, Esqs., *Wardens.* Rev. P. Phillips, *Minister and Secretary.*

W. LONDON SYNAGOGUE OF BRITISH JEWS, 34, Upper Berkley Street, Portman Square.

Wardens: C. G. Montefiore, A. J. Waley and H. S. Samuel, Esqs. Frederick G. Henriques and B. Elkin Mocatta, Esqs., *Treasurers.* Rev. Prof. D. W. Marks, *Chief Min.* Rev. Morris Joseph, *Delegate Chief Min.* Rev. Isidore Harris, M.A., *Minister and Secretary.* I. Lazarus, *Beadle and Collector.*

LONDON.

Synagogal Directory of the Jews of Gt. Britain.

New Dalston Synagogue and Schools.
Birkbeck Road, Sandringham Road.

M. Freedman, *Pres.* Mr. Sonenstein, *Vice.* P. Sandground, *Treas.* D. Greenberg, *Hon. Sec.* S. Manus, *Superintendent and Collector.*

Finsbury Park Synagogue, 20, Portland Road.
Mr. Charles Abrahams, *Secretary.*

South East London Synagogue, Lausanne Road, Peckham, S.E.

Mr. A. Frank, *Pres.* Mr. M. L. Myers, *Vice.* Mr. A. Perels, *Treas.* Rev. N. Goldston, *Minister and Secretary.*

Synagogue for Hammersmith & W. Kensington.
J. M. Levy, Esq., *Chairman, Ashley House, Rivercourt Road, Hammersmith.* B. L. Cohen, Esq., *Treas., 30, Hyde Park Gardens.*

North West London Synagogue, Clifton Hall, York Road, Camden Road, N.W.
Revs. I. Friedlander, and S. Friedman, *Mins.*

HAMPSTEAD SYNAGOGUE.
Rev. A. A. Green, *Minister.*

FEDERATION OF SYNAGOGUES.
Rev. Dr. Lerner, *Chief Magid.*
S. Montagu, Esq., M.P., *Pres.* H. Landau, Esq. *Vice.* L. Reed and I. Weber, Esq., *Treas.*

SPITAL SQUARE SYNAGOGUE, 10-11, Spital-sq.
J. M. Bœkbinder, Esq., *Pres.* S. Wallach, Esq, *Vice.* J. Bermel and J. B. Wechler, Esqs., *Wardens.* Rev. Ben Mosshe, *Reader.* Jos. E. Blank, *Sec.* M. Cohen, *Collector.*

POLISH SYNAGOGUE, Carter Street, Houndsditch.
J. Sternheim and H. Swalf, Esqs., *Wardens.* J. Bronkhorst, Esq., *Reader.* Mr. S. Bronkhorst, *Sec.* Mr. S. Weil, *Collector.*

LONDON.

Synagogal Directory of the Jews of Gt. Britain.

WILNA SOCIETY, 23, Fieldgate St., Whitechapel.

Mr. Levy, *Hon. Sec.*, 2, *Spelman Street, E.*

CRACOW BENEVOLENT SOCIETY AND SYNAGOGUE.

Mr. J. Singer, *President.* Mr. H. Rothman, *Vice-President.* Mr. H. Krautenfeld, *Treasurer.* Mr. S. Heiser, *secretary.* Mr. A. Woolf, *Collector.*

SCARBOROUGH STREET SYNAGOGUE.

H. Phillips, Esq., *Warden.* Mr. L. Phillips, *Hon. secretary.*

SANDY'S ROW SYNAGOGUE.

L. Reid, Esq., *President.* Jacob Fontyn, Esq., *Vice-President.* B. Woolf, Esq., *Treasurer.* J. Corper, *secretary.*

BROTHERS OF SUWALKI BENEFIT SOCIETY.

53, Hanbury Street, Spitalfields.

B. Abrahams, Esq., *President.* B. Landy, Esq., *Vice-President.* I. Lightstone, Esq., *Treasurer.* B. Israel, J. Zachar, A. Barnett, *Trustees.* I. Wolf and M. Cohen, *Wardens.* J. Levy, *Hon. secretary.*

MILE-END-NEW-TOWN SYNAGOGUE,

39, Dunk-street, E.

M. Michaels, Esq., *President.* J. Liebgott, Esq., *Vice-Pres.* I. Lazarus aud H. Dywin, *Wardens.* B. Freedman, Esq., *Treasurer.* H. Klott, *Beadle and Collector.*

PRESCOTT STREET SYNAGOGUE.

B. Van Staveren, Esq., *President.* M. Van Leer, Esq., *Vice-President.* E. Berg, Esq., *Treasurer.*

LOVERS OF PEACE, Tewkesbury Buildings, Whitechapel.

M. De Leef, Esq., *President.* Gabriel Haring, Esq., *Treasurer.* Isaac Klein, *secretary.*

LONDON.

Synagogal Directory of the Jews of Gt. Britain.

RIGHTEOUS PATH No. 2, 1, Catherine Wheel Alley, Bishopsgate.
J. Kaufmann, *secretary.*

LOVERS OF JUSTICE AND PEACE.
Green Man, Mansell Street.

J. Lœzen, *President.* I. L. Defries, *secretary and Collector, 10, Tenter Street, N. Goodman's Fields.*

BIKUR CHOLIM, 16, New Court, Fashion Street.

R. Joseph, Esq., *President.* H. Crown and P. Krotowsky, Esqs., *Wardens.* A. Salomons, Esq., *Treasurer.* A. R. Palache, *secretary.* G. Cohen, *Collector, 46, Gower's Walk.*

RECEIVERS OF PEACE, 18, Princes Street, Spitalfields.

J. Davidson, *President,* C. Angel and Ph. Silverstone, Esqs., *Wardens.* M. Joel, Esq., *Treasurer.* A. Heiser, *secretary.*

UNITED KALLISHER CONGREGATION,
Tenter Buildings, Goodmam's Fields.

L. Opper, Esq., *President.* R. Cohen, Esq., *Hon. Secretary.*

TEHELIM & MISHMORIM, Held at Princes-st. Synagogue.

M. Moses, Esq., *President.* J. Davidson, Esq., *Treasurer.* H. Levy and M. Barnett, Esq., *Wardens.* I. Kaliski, *Sec.*

SONS of PLOTZKAR, Held at Camperdown House, Half-moon Passage, Whitechapel.

J. Schonman, *President.* L. Goschewsky, *Treasurer.* S. Heiser, *Secretary.*

PEACE AND TRUTH, 113, Old Castle-street, Whitechapel.

M. Moses, Esq., *President.* H. Green, Esq., *Treasurer.* S. Michaels and S. Deyong, Esqs., *Wardens.* I. Kaliski, *Secretary.*

LONDON.

Commercial Directory of the Jews of Gt. Britain.

High Holborn.

Barnett, B., 319. Pawnbroker,

Bernstein, Ph., 285. Optician.

Cohen & Charles, 11, Thavies Inn. Wholesale manufacturing jewellers and diamond mounters. Importers of Continental jewelry.

Danziger, Adolph, 21, (City Temple.) Diamond merchant.

Davis, Alfred, 72. "Old Red Lion."

Davis & Sons, 316-18. Linen draper.

De Meza, J. & Sons, 122. Tobacconists.

Feldenheimer & Co., 21, (City Temple). Diamond merchants.

Isaacs, Alex,. 337. Hatter and trunk maker.

Jacobs, David, 190. Coffee-rooms.

Joseph Bros., 28, (Viaduct). Diamond merchants.

Kahn & Co., nr. Thavies Inn. Complete house-furnishers.

Lazarus, J. & Son, 67. High-class tailors.

Levy, M. J. & Nephews, 21, (City Temple). Diamond merchants.

Lyon, R., 124. Dealer in silverplate.

Mayers Bros., 203. High-class tailors.

LONDON.

Commercial Directory of the Jews of Gt. Britain.

Phillips, Ed., 286. Dentist.

Phillips, S. E. & L., 250. High-class tailors.

Wertheimer & Hirschhorn, 6, (Circus). Jewelry manufacturers.

High Street, Aldgate.

Greenbaum, P. & Son, 27; Manufacturing jewelers and diamond mounters.

Levy, Joseph, 79, 80-1; Tailor and hosier.

Phillips, H., 28; House furnisher.

Pozner, A. L., 32; Bespoke tailor.

High Street. Whitechapel.

Abrahams & Gluckstein, 26 and 120; Cigar manufacturers and tobacconists.

Bernstein, P., 76, and 1, Piccadilly, W., Importer of the Columbian jewelry.

Kams, M., 64; Passenger agent and bespoke tailor.

Houndsditch.

Abrahams, B., 115. Government store dealer.

Abrahams, Barnett A., Star Silver Depot. Wholesale jeweler etc.,

Abrahams, H. A. & Sons, 65: Novelties.

Abrahams, S. & Sons, 136; Wholesale jewelers and ring, keeper and chain manufacturers.

LONDON.

Commercial Directory of the Jews of Gt. Britain.

Bauman, N. & Co., 33; Wholesale and exportation cigars and cigarette manufacturers.

Benjamin, A. J., 150. Solicitor.

Britton, Joseph A., 16 & 18; Wholesale picture-frame manufacturer and printseller.

Cohen, I. & M., 53-4; Sponge merchant.

Costa Da, Barnett, 30, Cutler street. Wholesale cltohier and commission agent and job buyer.

Defries, & Sons. China merchants and lamp manufacturers.

Glensnick, J. & Son, 92; Manufacturers of clothing and woolens.

Green, J., 90. Boot and shoe manufacturer.

Greenholz, H., cor. Cutler. Manufacturing furrier. Fine assortment of furs always on hand.

Harris, H. S.. 116; Dealer in watches, jewelry and precious stones.

Harris, S., 154-5. Bead merchant.

Hart, Albert, 135. Hats and caps.

Hirsch, J., 105-6. China and fancy warehouse.

Hofman, S., 9; Toy warehouse.

LONDON.

Commercial Directory of the Jews of Gt. Britain.

Hyman, J. and Co., 54 and 103.   Military store dealers.

Isaacs, H. & Sons, 25, Cutler Street.   Wholesale and retail picture-frame manufacturers and dealers in works of art.

Isenstein, and Co., 120.   Importers of fancy goods.

Jacob, B., 21.   Shell importer.

Jacobs, A., 41; Wholesale hat and cap manufacturer.

Jacobs, S., 107-8.   Clothier.

Jacobs & Woolf, 55.   Fancy goods dealer.

Joseph, S., 10; Wholesale and retail ladies' tailor and mantle manufacturer.

Joseph, Samuel, 2, Harrow Alley.   Wholesale and retail clothier and job buyer.

Koski, C., 35.   Wholesale clothier.

Lesser, S., 24.   Birmingham warehouse.

Levy, N. & Sons, 11; Wholesale boot and shoe manufacturers, and leather merchants.

Marks, S. & Sons, 72.   Wholesale stationers.

Meyer, M., 57.   Job warehouseman.

Meyer, M. H., 156.   Foreign goods importer.

Misener, H. & Co., 90.   Mantle manufacturers.

LONDON.

Synagogal Directory of the Jews of Gt. Britain.

SUPPORTERS OF THE LAW.
Mr. I. Cohen, *President.* Mr. A. Smith, *Treasurer.*

SOCIETY COLONIZATION OF PALESTINE,
Held at the Jewish Working Men's Club,
Gt. Alie-street, E.

Mr. Kaufman, *Financial Secretary.*

PROVINCIAL SYNAGOGUES, OFFICIALS, &c.

BELFAST—Hebrew Congregation—Otto Jaffé, Esq., *Secretary,* Donegall-square, *South.*

BIRMINGHAM—Singer's-hill. Moses Berlyn, Esq., *Secretary, Synagogue-house, Singer's-hill.*

BLACKBURN, LANCS.—

BOSTON, LINCOLN—Mr. Canin, *Secretary, 37, Wide Bargate.*

BRIGHTON—Middle-street. Rev. A. C. Jacobs, *Secretary, Synagogue-chambers, Middle-st.*

BRISTOL—Park-row. Rev. A. H. Eisenberg, *Secretary, Synagogue-house, Park-row.*

CANTERBURY—King-street. Michael Abrahams, Esq., *Sec. 36, High-st.*

CARDIFF—East Terrace. Louis Barnett, Esq., *Secretary, 36, Charles-st.*

CHATHAM—Memorial Synagogue, Saint Margaret's-bank, Rev. Bernard J. Salomons, *Minister and Sec., 24, High-st., Rochester.*

CHELTENHAM—St. James'-square. J. Woolfe, Esq., *Secretary 7, Colonnade.*

CORK—

COVENTRY—Barras-lane. A. E. Friedlander, Esq., *Secretary, Cambridge-villa, Holyhead-road.*

LONDON.

Synagogal Directory of the Jews of Gt. Britain.

DOVER—Northampton-street. Rev. I. Bernstein, *Minister, Registrar and Secretary, Mildmay-lodge, Folkestone-road.*

DUBLIN New Hebrew Congregation—Mary's Abbey. Rev. Israel Leventon, *Secretary, 24, Emorville-avenue, South Circular-road.*

DUNDEE.—

EDINBURGH—Park-place. Henry Abrams, Esq., *Secretary, 14, Frederick-st.*

GLASGOW—Thistle-st., Garnett-hill. Michael Simons, Esq. *Secretary, 206, Bath-st.*

GRIMSBY—M. Abrahams, Esq., *Secretary, 86, Cleethorpe-road.*

HANLEY—Hanover-street, Adolph Alexander, Esq., *Secretary. 4, Market-sq.*

HULL—Robingon Row. L. H. Bergmon, Esq., *Secretary, 24, Waterworks-st.*

LEEDS—Rev. L. H. Forleser, *Secretary, 3, Northfield-villas.*

LEEDS—(New Briggate). Z. Wolfe, Esq., *Secretary, 77, Cobourg-st., Woodhouse-lane.*

LEICESTER—Crafton Street. L. L. Hyam, Esq., *Secretary, 19½, High-street.*

LIVERPOOL—(Old)—Princess Road. Rev. H. M. Silver, *Sec., 88, Falkner-st.*

LIVERPOOL—(New) Hope-place. Hyman Moses, Esq., *Sec., 37, Berkley-st., Princess-rd.*

MARGATE Hebrew Congregation. Freemason's-hall, High-st. E. I. Samuels, *Hon. Sec., Station Hotel.*

MANCHESTER— York-street, Cheetham. N. H. Harris, Esq., *16, Broughton-st., Cheetham.*

MANCHESTER—(South). Rev. I. Simon, *Sec., 114, Rumford-st., Chorlton-on-Medlock.*

MANCHESTER—Congregation of British Jews, Park-place, Cheetham.—Salis Simon, I. Frankenburg & J. Bauer, Esqs. *Wardens.* I. Danziger and Louis Scholes, *Treasurers.* Rev. L. M. Simmons, B.A., *Minister.* Isaac A. Isaacs, *Secretary.*

LONDON.

Synagogal Directory of the Jews of Gt. Britain.

MANCHESTER—Congregation of Spanish and Portuguese Jews. Nessim B. Messulam, Esq., *President.* Habib Ades, Esq. *Vice-pres.* Sabbato Levy, Esq., *Treasurer.* Rev. J., Valentine, *Reader.* David Davies, Esq., *Secretary, 15 Elizabeth-st, Cheetham.*

MERTHYR TYDVIL—Church-street. I. L. Jacobs, Esq., *sec., 38, Wellington-st.*

MIDDLESBORO'-ON-TEES Hebrew Congregation—Brentnall St., B. Nelson, Esq., *secretary, 68, Corporation-road.*

NEWCASTLE-ON-TYNE—United, Temple-st. Rev. L. Mendelson, B.A., *secretary, 26, Lawton-st.*

NEWPORT. (Mon).—Lewis-st. A. J. Jacobs, Esq., *secretary, 13, Cardiff-rd.*

NORTH SHIELDS—Linskill-st. J. M. Fisher. Esq., *secretary, 71, Clive-st.*

NORWICH.—St. Faith-lane. Heim Neumann, Esq., *secretary, Synagogue-house.*

NOTTINGHAM—7, George Street, Lesser Levy, Esq., *secretary, 34, George-st.*

PENZANCE—New-street. Israel H. Levin, Esq., *secretary, 8, The Terrace.*

PLYMOUTH.—9, Catherine- street. Rev. A. N. Spier, *secretary, Synagogue-house.*

PONTYPRIDD.—Taff-street. Marks Freedman, Esq., *secretary.*

PORTSEA.—Queen-street. Rev. Isaac Phillips, *secretary, Synagogue-house.*

RAMSGATE.—Hereson. Jacob Tritsch, Esq., *secretary, Hereson-House, St. Laurence-on-sea.*

SHEFFIELD.— North Church-st. Samuel Cohen, Esq., *secretary, 12, Corporation-st.*

SOUTHAMPTON.—Albion-place. Nathan Levy, Esq., *secretary, 21, Bridge-st.*

SOUTHPORT—Lionel Moss, Esq., *secretary, 36, Oak-street.*

STOCKTON-ON-TEES.—Skinner-street. A. Michelson, Esq., *secretary, 1, Central-buildings.*

LONDON.

Synagogal Directory of the Jews of Gt. Britain.

STOCKPORT—D. Bowman, Esq., *secretary*, 7, *Hindley-street, Hillgate.*

STROUD.—J. M. Shane, Esq.

SUNDERLAND—Moor-street. Edward George Asher, Esq., *secretary, 46, Frederick-st.*

SWANSEA—Isaac Seline, Esq., *secretary, 39, High-st.*

TREDEGAR—Marks J. S. Lyons, Esq., *secretary, 13, Commercial St., Ebbw-vale, near Tredegar.*

WEST·HARTLEPOOL—Abraham Harris, Esq., *secretary, 24, Church-st.*

WOLVERHAMPTON—Friar-street. Zachariah Wise, Esq., *sec., 7, Sidney-st.*

YORK—J. Rudolph, *secretary, The Terrace, Gillygate.*

LONDON.
Synagogal Directory of the Jews of Gt. Britain.
LIST of COLONIAL CONGREGATIONS
Under the jurisdiction of the Rev. the Chief Rabbi.

Congregation.	Minister.
ADELAIDE (South Australia) ..	Rev. A. F. Boas
AUCKLAND (New Zealand)	Rev. S. Goldstein
BALLARAT (Victoria)	Rev. J. M. Goldreich
BARBERTON (South Africa)	Rev. P. Wolfers
BRISBANE (Queensland)	Rev. P. Phillips
BURGERSDORP (Eastern Province, Cape Colony)	
CAPE TOWN (Cape Colony)	Rev. A. F. Ornstein
CHRISTCHURCH (New Zealand) ..	Rev. A. T. Chodowsky
DUNEDIN OTAGO (New Zealand) ..	Rev. B. Lichtenstein
GEELONG (Victoria)	
GRAHAM'S TOWN (Cape Colony) ..	
GRIQUALAND W. Kimberley (S. Africa)	Rev. Harris Isaacs
HOBART TOWN (Tasmania)	
JOHANNESBERG (S. Africa)	Rev. M. L. Harris
KINGSTON (Jamaica)	Rev. S. Jacobs
MELBOURNE (Victoria) Shearith Yisrael	Rev. Dr. J. Abrahams
Mikvch Yisrael ..	Rev. I. Myers
St. Kilda	Rev. E. Blaubaum
MONTREAL (Canada)	Rev. M. Friedlander
NELSON (New Zealand)	
OUDTSHOORN (South Africa) ..	Rev. M. Woolsohn
PORT ELIZABETH (Cape Colony) ..	Rev. S. Rapaport
QUEBEC (Canada)	
SANDHURST (Victoria)	Rev. Goldstone
SYDNEY (New South Wales).. ..	Rev. A. B. Davis
TIMARIS (Canterbury, N.Z.)	
TOOWOOMBA (Queensland)	Rev. Jacob Levy
TORONTO (Canada)	Rev. B. Elzas
WELLINGTON (New Zealand) ..	Rev. H. Van Staveren
WINNIPEG	Rev. D. Freedman

LONDON.

Charitable Directory of the Jews of Gt. Britain.

TEHELIM, MISHMORIM & BIKUR CHOLIM,
Held at Old Castle-street Synagogue.

S. Deyong, Esq., *President.* I. Cooper, Esq., *Vice-President.* S. Michaels, and W. Joseph, Esqs., *Wardens.* M. Isaacs, Esq., *Treasurer.* I. Kaliski, *Secretary.*

LOVERS OF PEACE, 90, Bridge-st., Burdett-rd., Mile End, E.

N. Spiro, Esq., *President.* Morris Abrahams, Esq., *Warden.* Rev. A. J. Miller, *Lecturer.* H. Bronkhorst, *Hon. Sec.*

CRACOW JEWISH FRIENDLY SOCIETY, held at Angel and Crown, High-street, Whitechapel.

J. Kaufman, *President.* W. Weber, *Vice-President.* M. Auerbach, *Treasurer.* S. Heiser, *Secretary.*

New West-end Religious Class in connection with the New West-end Synagogue, under the direction of the Rev. S. Singer.
SOUTH HACKNEY SYNAGOGUE & SABBATH SCHOOL,
43, Darnley Road, Devonshire Road, Mare Street.

A. B. Salmon, *President.* L. Zachariah, *Vice-President.* M. J. Heilbron, *Secretary.*

CONFINED MOURNING BENEFIT SOCIETY,
Held at the Carter-st. Synagogue.

L. Phillips, Esq., *President.* I. Levy, *Treasurer.* A. Prins, *Secretary.*

48, Hanbury-st., Spitalfields.

A. Simon, *President.* A. Goldman, *Treasurer.* B. Rosenthal and H. Cohen, *Wardens.* A. Heiser, *Secretary.*

GRACE & TRUTH, 40, Newcastle-st., Whitechapel

Mr. Hyman Green, *President.* Mr. Solomon Walter, *Treas.* Abraham Schmeldowski, *Secretary.*

HELPING HAND INCURABLE PENSION SOCIETY.

S. G. Risch, *President.* M. Roos, *Treasurer.*

LONDON.

Charitable Directory of the Jews of Gt. Britain.

Jewish Mutual Birmingham Benefit Society.
Nathan Nathan, President. Saul Lyons, Treasurer. L. Levy, Secretary.

Loyal United Friends' Friendly Society, 18, Princes-st.
J. Davidson, President. F. Falkenstein, Vice-President. M. Joel, Treasurer. I. Bloomfield, Secretary.

Jewish Communal League, Henage-lane, Bevis Marks.
Patron; Dr. Gaster. Manuel Castello, Esq., President. A. D. Martin, Hon. Sec., 15, Shepherd Street, E.

Birmingham Philanthropic Society.
P. H. Levi, President. M. Levenberg, Treasurer. M. Berlyn, Secretary.

Society for allowing Marriage Fees and a Portion.
L. M. Myers, Esq., President.

BENEVOLENT SOCIETIES, &c.

Board of Guardians for the Relief of the Jewish Poor.
13, Devonshire Square, Bishopsgate.

Benj. L. Cohen, Esq., President. The Right Hon. the Lord Mayor and F. D. Mocatta, Esqs., Vice-Presidents. F. A. Lucas and Leopold de Rothschild, Esqs., Treasurers. Lionel L. Alexandra, Esq., Hon. Secretary. M. Stephany, Secretary.

Spanish and Portuguese Board of Guardians.
Jos. de Castro, Esq., President. Frederick B. Halford, Esq., Treasurer.

LONDON.

Charitable Directory of the Jews of Gt. Britain.

Ladies' Association, Rosaline House, Tenter Street, North.

Lady Rothschild, President. Mrs. Cyril Flower, Hon. Sec. Mrs. Jones, Matron.

Western Jewish Philanthropic Society, St. Alban's Place.

Rev. L. Canter, Hon. Secretary.

Hand-in-Hand Benevolent Society, Cardiff.

Wm. L. Hegelstone, Esq., President. H. Goldman, Esq., Treasurer. S. M. Abrahams, Esq., Hon. Secretary.

Society for Relieving the Indigent Jewish Blind.

David Hyam, Esq., Treasurer. Mr. Henry H. Hyams, Sec.

Aged Needy Society.

For Pensioning Members of the Jewish Faith, who have attained the age of 60.

Lionel L. Alexander, Esq., President. H. Solomon and J. Cashmore, Esqs., Treasurers. M. H. Levirton, Esq., Hon. Sec. Mr. I. Bloomfield, Sec.

Assisting Society.

Joseph de Castro, Esq., President. Wolf Myers, Treasurer. I. A. Joseph, Vice-President and Hon. Secretary. H. H. Hyams, Secretary.

Five Shilling Sabbath Charity.

Joseph Montefiore Sebag, Esq., J.P., President. H. Jacob, Esq., Treasurer. Rev. M. Keizer, Secretary.

For Granting Loans to the Industrious Poor.

M. Castello, Esq., President. Mr. E. H. Lindo, Secretary.

Society for Granting Marriage Portions to Orphan Girls.

J. Montefiore Sebag, Esq., J.P., Treasurer. Edward Foligno and Elias H. Lindo, Esqs., Administrators.

LONDON.

Charitable Directory of the Jews of Gt. Britain.

Liverpool Hebrew Charities.

Charles S. Samuell, Esq., President.   Alfred L. Benas, Treas.

Ladies' Hebrew Benevolent Society, Middlesboro'

Mr. M. N. Bernstein, President.   Mrs. Hush, Treasurer.   Mrs. Phillips, Secretary.

Friend in Need Society, Middlesboro.'

Mr. I. Hush, President.   Mr. Getz, Treasurer.

Dublin Hebrew Philanthropic Society.

M. de Govot, President.   Charles L. Rus, Treasurer.

Hebrew Ladies' Benevolent Society, Melbourne.

Mrs. Simon Moss, President.   Mrs. E. P. Levy, Treasurer.   L. Pulver, Secretary.

Nottingham Philanthropic Society.

Albert Kahn, President and Treasurer.   J. Kramrisch, Hon. Secretary.

Society for Granting Marriage Portions & Relieving Poor Persons in Confined Mourning.

Moses Aflalo, Esq., Treasurer.   Mr. Jacob J. Hyam, Secretary.

Israelite Marriage Portion Society, 18, Princes-st.

L. Marchant, Esq., President.   Samuel Montagu, Esq., M.P., F. Wooton Isaacson, Esq., M.P., and D. Seroka, Esq., Vice-Presidents.   C. Angel, Esq., Treasurer.   I. Kaliski, Secretary.

Central Marriage Portion Society.

3 and 7, New Road, E.

L. Cohen, President.   J. Kaufman, Secretary, 3, Well St., E.

Ladies' Charity.

Mrs. F. D. Goldsmid, President.   Miss Toledana, Hon. Sec.

LONDON.

Charitable Directory of the Jews of Gt. Britain

Ladies' Benevolent Loan and Visiting Society.
Office—5, Duke Street, Aldgate.

Dowager Lady de Rothschild, President. Mrs. A. Strauss and Mrs. H. E. Symons, Treasurers. Mr. Henry H. Hyams, Serretary.

Society for Penny Dinners for Jewish Children.
Mrs. Birnbaum, Treasurer. Miss Birnbaum, Hon. Secretary. Miss Barnett, Superintendent, 5, Queen's Square, W.C.

West Central Jewish Relief Society.
B. Marcus, President. Rev. H. Davids, Treasurer. S. Levene, Hon. Sec.

Society for Providing Strangers with Meals on Sabbaths and Holydays.
I. Birnbaum, Esq., President. I. Levy, Vice-President. I. Weber, Esq., Treasurer. Mr. H. Smith, Secretary.

Lying-in-Charity.
Mr. Lionel Lucas, Hon. Secretary.

Jewish Emigration Society, 5, Duke-st., Aldgate.
Leopold de Rothschild, Esq., President. Walter Josephs, Esq., Treasurer. Mr. G. L. Lyons, Secretary.

Soup Kitchen, Fashion-street, Spitalfields.
Alfred L. Cohen, Esq., President. B. Birnbaum, Esq., Treas. Barrent S. Ellis, Esq., Hon. Secretary.

Stepney Jewish Benevolent Society.
H. Hymans, Esq., President. E. J. Proops, Esq., Vice-Pres.

East London Orphan Aid Society.
Rev. J. F. Stern and J. M. Lissack, Junr., Esq., Hon. Sec.

Shomre Shabbos Society.
Mr. L. Harris, Treasurer. Mr. Simmons, Hon. Sec., Rev. Dr. M. Lerner, Advocate.

LONDON.

Charitable Directory of the Jews of Gt. Britain.

Social Union Friendly Society.
Joseph Davis, Esq., President. S. Hess, Esq., Treasurer.

City of London Jewish Tailors' Benefit Society.
Held at the Horse and Trumpeter, Jewry Street, Aldgate.
G. Wortman, Esq., President. J. Albert, Esq., Treasurer. S. Heiser, Secretary.

Society of Promoters of Charity.
C. M. Nathan, Esq., President. Asher Isaacs, Esq., Vice-President. Moss, Benjamin, Esq., Treasurer. M. Cohen, Secretary.

Portsea Hebrew Benevolent Society:
Mr. M. Hart, President.

Jewish Tradesmen's Benevolent Society.
L. H. Phillips, C.C. President. L. M. Myers, Treasurer.

Cracowers Benevolent Society, Manchester.
W. Rothband, President. S. Papman, Treasurer. L. Rothband, Hon. Secretary.

Jewish Board of Guardians, Leeds.
M. Zanenberg, President. M. Cohen, Treasurer. J. Blasbker and N. Zanenberg, Hon. Secretaries.

Birmingham Hebrew Board of Guardians.
Mr. A. Bremer, President. Mr. P. H. Levi, Treasurer.

Surrey Philanthrophic Society, Heygate Street, Walworth, S.
I. Davis, Esq., President. Mr. B. Solomons, Secretary.

Jewish National Association, 45, Gt. Prescott-st., E.
P. J. Solomons, Esq., President. S. Isaacs, Esq., Vice-Pres. A. A. Romain, Esq., Treasurer. J. Hart, Secretary. L. E. Levene and B. Schaap, Collectors.

LONDON.

Charitable Directory of the Jews of Gt. Britain.

Matzo Association, Sydney, Capital, £3000.

Philanthropic Society for Relieving Distressed Widows
with £13 per annum for life.
A. Rosenfeld, Esq., President.   I. M. Marks, Esq., Vice-Pres.
Jacob Levy, Esq., Treasurer.   I. J. Abrahams, Hon. Sec.

Loyal Independent Lodge of Good Fellows, No. 2.
Myer Fox, President.   W. Phillips, Treasurer.   L. Levy, Sec.

Path of Righteousness Benefit Society.
H. L. Harris, President.   Lewis Van Praagh, Treasurer.
L. Levy, Secretary.

The Children's Country Holiday Fund.
Ernest L. Franklin, Esq., President.

LONDON.

Club Directory of the Jews of Gt. Britain.

Association for the Diffusion of Religious Knowledge.

N. S. Joseph & S. Montagu, M.P., Presidents. E. A. Franklin, Vice-President. H. Lucas, Treasurer. Rev. M. Joseph, J. A. Franklin and H. Kisch, Esqs., Hon. Secs.

Anglo-Jewish Historical Society.

Joseph Jacobs and Lucien Wolf, Esqs., Hon. Secs.

Girls' Club, 33, Devonshire Street, W.C.

Miss Emily Harris, Promoter.

Jewish Girls' Club, 22, Gt. Prescott Street, E.

Mrs. Louis Davidson, President. Lady Magnus, Treasurer. Miss E. Gollancz, Hon. Secretary.

Cardiff Jewish Literary and Musical Institute.

Rev. J. H. Landau, Founder.

Hebrew Dramatic Club, 3, Princes Street, Spitalfields.

W. Smith, Manager. I. Kaliski, Secretary.

Jewish Working Men's Club.

Samuel Montagu, Esq., M.P., President. Stuart M. Samuel and Lionel L. Alexander, Esqs., Vice-Presidents.

Sir Moses Montefiore Literary and Art Society.

Tavistock Place, W.C.

Mr. I. Abrahams, F.R.S.L., President. Mr. W. L. Shepherd, M.R.C.S., S.S.A., Vice-President. Mr. H. Lawrence, F.S.S., Director. H. Myers, Hon. Secretary. Mr. E. P. Abrahams, Musical Director.

Manchester Jewish Working Men's Club, 4, York St.

A. R. Besso, Esq., President. L. Lichtenstein, Esq., Vice-President.

LONDON.

Collegiate Directory of the Jews of Gt. Britain

SCHOOLS, COLLEGES & LITERARY SOCIETIES.

Jews' College, Tavistock House, Tavistock Square, W.
Rev. Dr. Herman Adler, Chief Rabbi, President. Michael Friedlander, Ph.D., Principal. H. Solomon and C. Samuels, Esqs., Treasurers. H. H. Hyams, Secretary.

Rabbinical College, James' Place, Aldgate.
Rev. B. Spiers, Doyen.

Provincial Jewish Ministers' Fund—Donations solicited by
S. Montagu, Esq., M.P., President. B. L. Cohen, Esq., Treas. Stuart M. Samuel, Esq., Hon. Sec.

Keshaim College, Heneage Lane.
D. de Pass, Esq., Treasurer. J. Afriat, Esq., Warden. Mr. Samuel I. Cohen, Secretary.

Lady Judith Montefiore's Theological College, Ramsgate.
Rev. Dr. Gaster, Principal.

Aria College, Portsea.
Dr. W. Stern, Principal. Mr. John Edwards, Secretary, 70, Union Street, Portsea.

North London Beth Hammedrash.
127, Newington Green Road. A. L. Sions, Hon. Sec.

Jews' Free School, Bell Lane, Spitalfields.
The Right Honorable Lord Rothschild, President. A. L. Cohen, Esq., Treasurer. Mr. M. Duparc, Secretary.

Jews' Infant School, Commercial Road, Whitechapel.
Sir Julian Goldsmid, M.P., President. F. D. Mocatta, Esq., Vice-President. L. Van Oven, Esq., Treasurer. Walter Josephs, Hon. Secretary. Mr. Alfred Henry, Secretary. Miss E. M. Betteridge, Head Mistress.

LONDON.

Collegiate Directory of the Jews of Gt. Britain.

Jewish Male Adult School, held at the Jews' Free School.
Supported by the late Baroness Lionel de Rothschild, M. Angel, Esq., Superintendent.

Gates of Hope Incorporated School, Heneage Lane.
Elias De Pass, Esq., President, J. N. Castello, Junr., Esq., Treasurer. Mr. S. I. Cohen, Secretary.

Infant School, Heneage Lane, Bevis Marks.
Mrs. Almosnino, President. Miss A. J. De Pass, Hon. Sec.

Villareal Girls' School.
Miss G. Lindo, Treasurer. Alice J. De Pass, Hon. Secretary.

Borough Jewish Schools, Heygate Street, Walworth, S.
Arthur Cohen, Esq., Q.C., M.P., President. A. M. Sebag, Esq., Treasurer. R. Singer, Hon. Secretary.

Westminster Jews' Free Schools.
Hanway Place, W.

Louis Davidson, Esq., President. Claude G. Montefiore, Esq., Vice-President. Julian Joseph, Esq., Treasurer. Mr. J. Woolf, Secretary.

Bayswater Jewish School.
St. James' Terrace, Harrow Road, W.

J. Bertheil, Esq., President. Rev. R. Harris, Hon. Secretary.

Stepney Jewish Schools.
M. N. Adler, Esq., M.A., President. B. Kisch, Esq., Vice-President. A. Arnholz, Esq., Treasurer. Henry Hymans, Stephen S. Hyam and A. Morley, Esqs., Hon. Secs.

Old Ford Jewish Classes. Olga Street Board School.
S. Valentine, President. M. Davis, Vice-President. Mr. I. Bloomfield, Hon. Secretary. Mr. and Mrs. S. Heiser, Teachers.

Society of Hebrew Literature.
Joseph Jacobs, Secretary.

LONDON.

Hospital Directory of the Jews of Gt. Britain.

JEWISH HOSPITALS, ASYLUMS, &c.

Jews' Hospital & Orphan Asylum, Lower Norwood.
Dr. H. Behrend, President. Edward Davis, Esq., Vice-Pres. Edward Lucas and Daniel Marks, Esqs., Treasurers. M. J. Green, Secretary. M. Raphael, B.A., Head Master.

Jewish Home for Incurables, 49, Victoria Park Road.
Office—100c, Queen Victoria Street. M. Barnett, Hon. Sec.

Jews' Deaf and Dumb Home.
Walmer Road, Notting Hill, W. Sir Philip Magnus, President. Edward Stern, Esq., Treas. Rev. I. Samuel, Hon. Sec.

Spanish and Portuguese Jews' Orphan Institution.
9, Howley Place, Maida Hill, W.—Removed from Bevis Marks. D. De Pass, Esq., President and Treasurer. Mr. Samuel I. Cohen, Secretary. Mr. and Mrs. A. Talano, Master and Matron.

Spanish and Portuguese Hospital, Mile End.
Manuel Castello, Esq., Treasurer. Judah Piza, and Moses B. Levy, Esqs., Wardens. E. H. Lindo, Secretary.

Hand-in-Hand and Widows' Home Asylum, Well Street, Hackney.
Benjamin L. Cohen, Esq., President. John Harris and Wolfe Isaacs, Esqs., Vice-Presidents. Moses Davis and S. Pool, Esqs., Treasurers. I. Bloomfield, Secretary.

Jewish Home, 37 and 39, Stepney Green.
F. D. Mocatta, Esq., President. Barrow Emanuel, Esq., Vice-President. H. M. Harris and S. Silver, Esqs., Treasurers. I. Bloomfield, Secretary.

Jewish Convalescent Home.
Founded in Memory of Lady Judith Montefiore.
Portland Road, South Norwood.
G. S. Joseph and E. N. Adler, Esqs., Hon. Secretaries. Dr. Maurice Davis, Hon. Medical Attendant.

Poor Jews' Temporary Shelter, Leman Street, E.
Ellis A. Franklin, President. Samuel Montagu, Esq., M.P., Treasurer. B. Birnbaum and H. Landau, Esqs., Vice-Presidents. Harvey Samuel, Esq., Hon. Secretary.

LONDON.

Hotel Directory of the Jews of Gt. Britain.

Metropolitan & Provincial Hotels.

METROPOLITAN.

J. Cohen, 101, Hatton Garden.　L. Green, 109, Sutherland-av.
Mr. S. Solomons, 29, Cawley Road, Victoria Park, E.
Mrs. Samuels, 8, Woburn Place, Russell Square, W.C.
R. Clifford, 50, Strand.
Miss Alexander, 33, Montagu Place, Russell Square, W.C.
D. Goldstien, 5, Bloomfield Street, Finsbury.
Saunders, Camperdown House, Half-moon Passage, Gt. Alie-st.

PROVINCIAL.

BIRMINGHAM—D. Joseph, 29, Smallbrook Street.
　　　　　　Mrs. Raphael, 29, Newhall Hill Parade.
　　　　　　M. Nathan, Edgbaston Street.　Isaacs, Pershore-st.
　　　　　　M. Cohen, 84, Bristol Street.
BOURNEMOUTH—Clifton Hall.　Mrs. Harrison, West Cliff.
BRIGHTON—Miss Zapira, 14, Clarence Square.
　　　　　H. N. Hyman, 37, Regency Square.
　　　　　Regency House and Pier Mansion, King's Road.
　　　　　Mrs. Lion, (Joseph's) Oaklands, 8, Cavendish Place.
　　　　　Aquarium Hotel, Manchester Street.
　　　　　M. S. Nurenberg, 15 and 16, Devonshire Place.
　　　　　Levy, Valdivia House, Egremont Place.
　　　　　Mrs. Moss Heilbron, 35, Oriental Place.
　　　　　Malborough Mansions, 14 and 15, King's Road.
　　　　　Madame Scheyer, 17, Upper Rock Gardens.
CHATHAM—Rev. B. J. Salomons, Synagogue House.
EASTBOURNE—Miss Davis, 3, Silverdale Road.
EDINBURGH—Mrs. H. Joel, 36, Grindlay Street.
　　　　　　Mrs. Solomon, 3, Bristo Place.
HASTINGS—A. I. Joseph, 12, Roberston Terrace.
　　　　　Stone & Joseph, 19, Devonshire Road.
　　　　　C. A. Schawabe, Albany Hotel.
LIVERPOOL—J. Aarons, Benson Street.
　　　　　　R. N. Freedman, corner of Lord Nelson Street.
LLANDUDNO—Aarons, Ripon House, Gloddaeth Crescent.
　　　　　　M. Newton, Royal Crescent.
MARGATE—E. I. Samuels, Station Hotel.　Cliftonville Hotel.

LONDON.

Hotel Directory of the Jews of Gt. Britain.

MANCHESTER—Cohen, 150, York Street, Cheetham.
    Phillips & Co., 62, York Street, Cheetham.
    S. Delmar, 15,   d).,   do.
    Isaacs, Moreton Street, Strangeways.
    A. Lazarus, 32, York Street, Cheetham.
    S. Jacobs, New Bridge Street.
    Adutt, Strangeways.   Joseph, Strangeways.
    Cafe Royal, 51, Peter Street.
NEWCASTLE-ON-TYNE—Harris, 83, Carlisle Street.
OXFORD—Mrs. S. Hyamson, 47, Wellington Square.
PLYMOUTH—Joel, 15, Buckland Street.
PORTSEA—Phillis, Queen Street.
RAMSGATE—Solomon, 5, Victoria Parade.
    Misses Barnett, The Laurel Boarding House, 7,
    Mrs. da Costa, 10, do.   [Agusta Road.
    Shandel, 3 and 4, Arklow Square.
    Schwarzwald, Arklow Square.
ST. LEONARDS-ON-SEA—Jay, 69; Jacobs, 61; Hyman, 92,
    A. S. Hyamson, 39, Magdalen Road. [Warrior-sq.
SCARBOROUGH—J. Goldman, Clarendon House, 61, Queen's
SOUTHAMPTON—Grosbaum, 1, Brunswick Square. [Parade.
SOUTHPORT—Mrs. J. Lambert, Sorrento House, Knowsley-rd.
TEIGNMOUTH—Louis, Rose Hill Cottage, Bitten Street.

London Poultry Killers.

Messrs. Mesquita & Landau, 3, Tenter Street, E.

Schechita Board, Bevis Marks.

Mr. Samuel Montagu, M.P., President.   M. Castello, Vice-President.   Rev. I. Cohen, Secretary.   M. M. Vanthal, Investigating Officer.

MANCHESTER.

Commercial Directory of the Jews of Gt. Britain.

CHEETHAM-HILL ROAD.

Balint, Susman, 26a, Lord Street; Wholesale and retail cloth dealer.

Baum, A., 46, Lord Street; Baker, grocer and provision dealer.

Burman, H., 68; Cigar and cigarette importer.

Cohen, Harris, 27, Elizabeth street; Retail traveling jeweller.

Cohen, Henry, 47, Tailor and general draper.

Cohen, Jos., 36; Wholesale and retail spirits.

Davis, Levy, 34, Park Street; Tailor and general draper.

Dembowitch, Simon, 6, Clarence street; Butcher. Sausages and all kinds of smoked and pickled provisions supplied.

Erb, H. & Hyman, D., 14, Shaw Street; Wholesale and retail tailors.

Farber, Moses, 41a, Lord street; Tobacconist and cigarette manufacturer.

Falk, Harris, 28, Park street; Fashionable tailor, and tailoring for the trade.

Feinberg, H. M. 6, Robert Street; Cap manufacturer.

MANCHESTER.

Commercial Directory of the Jews of Gt. Britain.

Fletcher, David, 24, Adeline street; Wholesale boot shoe and slipper manufacturer.

Franks, M., 12, Robert Street; Cloth cap manufacturer.

Freedman, E., 4, Adeline street, Eton court; Wholesale cap manufacturer.

Friedland, L., 58a; Cheetham Tailoring Establishment.

Gilbert, I., 13b, Exchange street; Wholesale cabinet manufacturer.

Glaskie, Abm., 4, Clarence street; grocer and general provision dealer.

Glaskie, H & Co., 5, Adeline street; Wholesale and retail grocer, baker, and flour dealer, passover cake and provisions. Orders received.

Glodt, D., 42; Watchmaker and jeweller.

Goodman, Moses, Skip place, Park street; Tailor.

Gordon, Jos., 1c, Park street; Plain and fancy box manufacturer and draper.

Gottberg, J., 85; Lace merchant.

Harris, Hyman, 16 Adeline street; Wholesale boot shoe and slipper merchant.

Isaacs, Harris, 12, Robert street; Wholesale and retail tailor.

MANCHESTER.

Commercial Directory of the Jews of Gt. Britain.

Kimmelfeld, F., 5, Adeline street; cap-peak and blank manufacturer.

Latter, S., 82 ; Grocer and foreign provision dealer. Orders by post promptly attended to.

Lazarus, David, 32 ; Family and Temperance Hotel.

Levi, J., 45 ; General draper.

Levy, Jacob, 2. Adeline street; Butcher. Worsht and sausage manufacturer.

Light, Henry, 5, Bent terrace, Bent street; Watchmaker and jeweller for the trade.

Louis, Nathan, 1, Adeline street ; Grocer and dealer in smoked beef, wurst, and finest oils, Spanish olives, cucumbers, Dutch cheese, etc., established 1850.

Marks, A., 12, Robert street; Tailoring for the trade.

Marks, Morris, 63 ; Practical tailor and draper.

Mendel, I. & Son, 59 ; Watchmakers and jewellers for the trade.

Meyer, E., 70 ; Reliable watchmaker and jeweller. Country orders promptly attended to. Est. 1872.

MANCHESTER.

Commercial Directory of the Jews of Gt. Britain.

Morris, Eli, 11, Lord street; Baker, grocer, and general provision dealer. Matzos and Passover provisions.

Oleesky, Sam., 40; Wholesale and retail Hebrew and English bookseller. Silk and woollen Talaisim merchant.

Plotzker, Bernhard, 46; and 95, Strangeways; *Kosher* meat salesman, and German sausage manufacturer by gas power. Meat and sausages supplied at wholesale.

Plotzker, Jos., 79; and 179, Great Ducie Street, Strangeways; meat salesman, worsht and sausage manufacturer by gas power. Country orders at reasonable prices.

Raphel, Wm., 43; Cap manufacturer.

Ring, David, 27, Johnson street; Painter, paper-hanger and house-decorator.

Rosenfeld, S., 32, Park street; Dealer in general drapery and cotton, silk and linen thread.

Rosenthal Isaac, 8, Park Place; Restaurant.

Rotenberg, A., 15, Park street; Wholesale cap manufacturer.

Sclamberg, L., Exchange Street; Hat and cap manufacturer.

MANCHESTER.

Commercial Directory of the Jews of Gt. Britain.

Shemenski, N. & Co., 66a, Family boot and shoe warehouse. Repairs neatly done.

Shiers, S. & Co., 11, Exchange street; Jewellers and diamond dealers,

Vitofski, A., 41, Lord street; Wholesale and retail baker, grocer and provision dealer.

Vitofski, L., 51; Draper, jeweller and clothier.

Woolf, Hyman, 64; Wholesale and retail baker, grocer and foreign provision dealer. Choice Berlin Matzos and Passover provisions. Country orders attended to.

CORPORATION STREET.

Danziger, M. & J., 71; Merchants and Importers of fancy leather goods.

Finkelstein, Isaac, 118; Dealer in new and second-hand furniture. Weekly payments. Furniture bought, sold or exchanged.

Newman, M., 10 & 10a; Fine art dealer and printseller. Wholesale and retail.

Pareezer, Jac., 26, Fennel street; Clothing manufacturer and tailor for the trade.

Paskin, Harris, 70, Hanover street; Wholesale slipper manufacturer.

MANCHESTER.

Commercial Directory of the Jews of Gt. Britain.

Rottenberg, J., 76 and 62a, Hanover street; Wholesale grocer.

Weinstein, Morris, 172; Tailors' and cap-makers' trimmings and general cloth dealer.

COOPER STREET.

Cohen, Sig. Oppenheim & Co., 25; Shippers.

Rosenbloom, L. & Son, 36; Shippers.

Sternberg, Bros., 25: Shippers.

CUMBERLAND STREET.

Henriques & Co., Merchants and shippers.

DANTZIC STREET.

Cohen, B., 25, Mayes street; Manufacturer of waterproof garments.

Fletcher & Rosenberg, 12, Back Balloon street; Cap manufacturer.

Gotliffe, S. Lewis & Co., 13 and 15, Mayes street; Waterproof manufacturers.

Hersh, M., 7; Wholesale clothier.

Pavion, L. & Co., 10, Back Balloon street; Waterproof garment manufacturers.

HIGH STREET.

Aaronovitch, P., Friday street, wholesale fent dealer.

Ehrlich, H. & Co., 66a; Merchants.

MANCHESTER.

Commercial Directory of the Jews of Gt. Britain.

Goldsmith, I., 7, Nicholas Croft, op. Wellington Hotel; High-class tailor and outfitter.

Goodman, Jac. E., 24, Edge street; Wholesale clothier.

Jacobson, B., 17a and 29a, Turner street; Job and Fent merchant. Wholesale and retail dealer in woollens, calicoes, velvets, cashmeres, &c.

Kandel, Abm., 8a, Turner street; Job dealer.

King, L. & Co., 20, Thomas street; Cigar and cigarette manufacturer. London branch, Ludgate Arcade, Ludgate Hill.

Koffler, C. & Lazarus, 22a, High street; Job and fent merchants.

Landes & Reicher, 14a, Turner street; Job merchants.

Lobel, A., 12, Turner street; General job dealer.

Reicher, Ph., 46a; Wholesale and retail general warehouseman.

Ribatskie, D., 31a, Turner street; Job and fent dealer.

Rosenzweig, D. & Co., 7, Friday street; Fent merchants.

Sampson, Sampson, 38, Church street; Print merchant.

MANCHESTER.

Commercial Directory of the Jews of Gt. Britain.

Solomon, J. & Son., 20, Thomas street, Furriers.

Taylor, D., 16b. Church street; Manufacturer of aprons, pinafores, frocks, underclothing, &c. Country orders promptly attended to.

High Town.

Kolmer, Wm., 251, Waterloo road; New and second-hand furniture.

Levy, Marks, 71, Bell street; Butcher and sausage manufacturer.

Marks, E., 248, Waterloo road; Hairdresser and tobacconist.

Long Millgate.

Goldman, L., 1, Ashley lane, Derby court; Tailoring for the trade.

Klainman, P., 1, Ashley lane, Derby court; Wholesale cloth, silk and fancy cap manufacturer.

Libstein, Jac., Irk Mills; Boot and slipper manufacturer and leather merchant.

Marcus, Jac., Derby court Cabinet works; Repairs and alterations. Country orders promptly attended to.

Nathan, D., 1, Ashley lane, Derby court; Tailoring for the trade.

MANCHESTER.

Commercial Directory of the Jews of Gt. Britain.

Rosenbaum, S., 128; Waterproof garment manufacturer.

Rosenthal, D., 1, Ashley lane, Derby court; Tailoring for the trade.

LOWER BROUGHTON.

Balon, R., 28, Edward street; Tassel and trimming manufacturer.

MARKET STREET.

Alexander, A., 91: Merchant tailor.

Levien, Benj., 79; Tailor and draper.

Lewis's; Manufacturers and general merchants. Est. 1879. Liverpool and Birmingham.

Mandleberg, J., & Co., Ltd., The "Albion" waterproof works, Pendleton; and at 95 and 105a. Waterproof goods.

Moss, J. S. and Sons, 23; Wholesale and retail clothiers.

Samuel, H. and Son, 97 and 99. Offices, Marsden square; Watch manufacturers; wholesale and retail jewellers.

Sternberg, Nathan, 15; Silversmith and jeweller.

MILLER STREET.

Doniger, M., 18; Cap manufacturers.

MANCHESTER.

Commercial Directory of the Jews of Gt. Britain.

Ellison, L., Edward street; Wholesale cabinet manufacturer; Bedroom suites in American walnut, satin walnut, walnut and maple, ash, mahogany and deal, in newest designs.

Frankenstein, P. and Sons, 33; Manufacturers of rubber fabrics. Factories: Victoria rubber works, Newton Heath.

Ginsberg, I., 67 and 69; Wholesale and retail general draper and milliner.

Hildesheimer, S. and Co., Lt., 63; Manfs. mouldings picture frames, &c.

Marks, H., 25 : Wholesale cap manufacturer.

Mistovski, L. and Co., 59, 61, and 61a, ; India-rubber manufacturers. Works: The "Broadfield" rubber works, Heywood near Manchester.

Rosenthal, S., 27 : Wholesale cap manufacturer.

Singerman, S., Albert bldgs.: cap manufacturer.

NEW BRIDGE STREET.

Black, O., 5; Ladies' and Gents' bespoke tailor and tailoring for the trade.

Fraser, Barnet, 67; Ladies' and Gent's bespoke tailor, and tailoring for the trade.

Hoffman, Sam., 7a, Salford; Practical tailor.

MANCHESTER.

Commercial Directory of the Jews of Gt. Britain.

Wansker, Jos., 6, Dutton street; Tassel and trimming manufacturer.

Weiner, Sam., New Bridge street rubber works; Ladies' and Gents' vulcanised waterproof garments. Est. 1869.

OLDHAM ROAD.

Faust, Wm., 59, Tib street, Queen's bldgs.; Tailoring for the trade.

Koffman, Louis, 13, Henry street; Wholesale cabinet manufacturer.

PORTLAND STREET.

Behrens, Louis and Sons, 131; Merchants and manufacturers.

Ellinger, and Co., 127; Shipping merchants.

Hesse, Max. 4; Agent for foreign manfs.

Hirschberg and Co., 100; Merchants and manufacturers.

Langstein, M. and Co., 4; Printers.

Sassoon, David and Co., 113; Shipping merchants.

PRINCESS STREET.

Kaufman, L., 44; Merchant.

RED BANK.

Cohen, Louis, 43, Fernie street: Matzo baker, flour dealer and grocer.

MANCHESTER.

Commercial Directory of the Jews of Gt. Britain.

Friedman, A., 29, Verdon street; Wholesale clothier.

Sniderman, H. 47, Fernie street; Clothing and piece-goods.

Rochdale Road.

Kaufman, D,, 43, Cable street; Wholesale furniture manufacturer and warehouseman.

Salford.

Frankenburg, I.: Rubber fabrics.

Sieff, E., 52, Broughton road; Cotton and woollen rag merchant.

Sugarman, Nachman, 120, Greengate street; Picture-frame maker.

Shudehill.

Babrovskie, Weinberg and Co., 17, Bradshaw street: Waterproof manufacturers and leather goods.

Barder, A., 20, Thomas street; Manufacturer and importer of fancy leather goods. Bags, purses, albums, cigar and cigarette cases, fans, photo frames, &c.

Friesner, Emanuel, 39, Thomas street; Tailoring for the trade.

Friesner, L., 39, Thomas street Tailoring for the trade and clothing manufacturer.

MANCHESTER.

Commercial Directory of the Jews of Gt. Britain.

Goldman, M., 4, Dantzic street; Wholesale clothing manufacturer.

Jacobson, S., 22, Bradshaw street; Stay and corset manufacturer.

Levy, A., 42, Hanover street; Wholesale cap manufacturer.

Markus, Bernard, 6, New street; Waterproof garment manufacturer and leather goods.

Michaels, Israel and Co., 38, Dantzic street; Boot, shoe and slipper manufacturers.

Pavion Bros., 55, Hanover street ; Cap manufacturers.

Steel A., 8, Thomas street; importer of English and Geneva watches. Watchmakers' and jewellers' materials and tools.

STRANGEWAYS.

Backner, Carl, 121, Gt. Ducie street; Wholesale and retail tobacco and cigars.

Barron, J., 8, Bury New road; Wholesale and retail drapery.

Berman, M., 21, Bury New road; New and second hand furniture. Weekly payments taken.

Cohen, A., 37, Briddon street, Hat and cap manufacturer.

MANCHESTER.

Commercial Directory of the Jews of Gt. Britain.

Cohen, M., 15, Bury New road; *Kosher* butcher, sausages and all kinds of pickled and smoked provisions supplied.

Cohen. Sol., 76, Moreton street; Baker, grocer and general provision dealer.

Cornofsky, L., 22, Bury New road: Baker, grocer and general provision dealer.

Davis, Isaac, Room 27, Empire bldg., Moreton street; Tailoring for the trade.

Dovidovich, I,, 171, Gt.Ducie street; Manufacturer of aprons, pinafores, &c.

Dryer, Jac., & Co., 72, Moreton street; Loan office.

Feinberg, Jac, 107, Moreton street; Grocer and general provision dealer.

Feineman, H. 103, Moreton street; Custom tailor and tailoring for the trade.

Freedman, H. & Co., 37, Briddon street; Wholesale cap manufacturers.

Freizer, Morris, 8, Boundary street; Master tailor for the trade.

Frendt, A., 97, Gt. Ducie street; Practical tailoring and tailoring for the trade.

Gardie, M., 20, Bury New road; General grocer and provision dealer.

MANCHESTER.

Commercial Directory of the Jews of Gt. Britain.

Gilbert, S., 25, Briddon street; Master tailor for the trade.

Goldberg & Bloom, Room 40, Empire bldg., Moreton street; Tailoring for the trade.

Goldstone, Louis, Room 6, Empire bldg., Moreton street; Tailor and cloth merchant.

Goldwater, J., 132, Moreton street; Custom tailor and tailoring for the trade.

Green, Solomon, 91, Gt. Ducie street; Working jeweler, electro-plate gilder and tobacconist.

Hyman, A., 62, Gt. Ducie street; Baker and provision dealer, reliable matzo baker and Passover provisions.

Hyman, M., 81, Moreton street; General draper.

Kersh, J., 25, Briddon street; Master tailor for the trade.

Kolomer, Nathan, 18, Bury New road; Bedsteads and bedding, spring mattresses and upholsterer.

Koffler, Chas., 43, Julia street; Hat and cap manufacturer.

Landes, Max H., 14, Howard Street; General dealer in cashmeres, silks, velvets, &c.

Lang Bros. & Co., Briddon Street; Hat and cap manufacturers.

MANCHESTER.

Commercial Directory of the Jews of Gt. Britain.

Levene, Barnet, 83, Moreton street; Wholesale and retail tailors' trimmings.

Levinson, Simon, Room 9, Empire bldg., Moreton street; Rag merchant.

Lewis, Harris, 97, Moreton street; Master tailor for the trade.

Linskie, T., 26, Briddon street; Practical tailor.

Lipoloskie, I., 126, Moreton street; Baker, grocer and provision dealer, reliable matzo baker and Passover provisions.

Maimon, A. & Co., 43, Bury New road; Wholesale and retail provision merchants.

Nathan, F., 4, Southall street; Tailoring.

Nathan, N., 11, Moreton street; Wholesale cap manufacturer.

Normie Bros., 10, Little Bridge street; Wholesale cabinet manufacturers to the trade. Dining and bedroom suites, and kitchen furniture of every description of wood.

Plotzker, David, 179, Great Ducie street; Meat salesman, wurst, and sausage manufactured by gas power: special attention to country orders.

MANCHESTER.

Commercial Directory of the Jews of Gt. Britain.

Ranbach, M., 13, Nightingale street; and 25 and 43, Bury New road; Grocer and provision dealer. Dealer in all kinds of tailors' trimmings. Hebrew and English bookseller. Silk and woolen talaisim.

Rosenberg, D., Room 4, Empire bldg.; Wholesale cap manufacturer.

Sampson, Sol., 43, Bury New road; Choice greengrocer and provision merchant. Country orders received.

Simons, Jos., 101, Moreton street; Tailoring for the trade.

Stern, J., 38, Gt. Ducie street; Watchmaker, working jeweller and repairer of musical boxes.

Verberlovski, Ph., 8, Boundary street; Master tailor for the trade.

Wansker, Benj., 64, Moreton street; Trimming manufacturer.

Wiener, P. B., 4, Southall street; Waterproof manufacturer.

SUGAR LANE.

Meyerstone, H., 33, New Brown st.; Master tailor.

MANCHESTER.

Commercial Directory of the Jews of Gt. Britain.

Swan Street.

Goodman, I. & Co., 52; Complete house-furnisher.

Upton Street.

Elder, H. & Co., Victoria Quilt Co.

Victoria Street.

Aaronsberg, W. & Son, 12; Ophthalmic opticians. Instrument makers to Her Majesty the Queen.

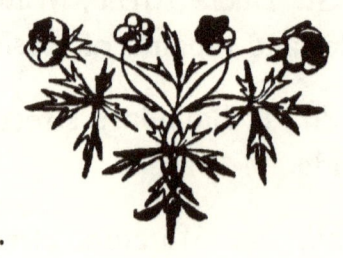

MIDDLESBROUGH.

Commercial Directory of the Jews of Gt. Britain.

ALBERT ROAD.

Benjamin, H.; Financial agent.
Franks, M.; Optician.
Goldseller, J.; Auctioneer and appraiser.
Phillips, J., Chatham Villas; Financial agent.
Phillips, Dr., Chatham Villas; Physician.
Reubens, Isaac, 47, Albert Mews; Slipper manfacturer.

BRIDGE STREET.

Levy, A., 26, 27 and 28; Clothier and jeweller.
Pinto, D.; General dealer.

CANNON STREET.

Hush, Isaac, 194; Pawnbroker and clothier.
Kaufman, S.; Boot and shoe dealer.
Levy, W., 10; Clothier and slipper manufacturer.
Marks, P.; General dealer.
Smollan, J.; Pawnbroker,
Wilkes, J., 165; Picture-frame and general dealer.

CORPORATION ROAD.

Behrman, Isaac, 26; Complete house-furnisher.
Jacobs, Maurice, 75; Pawnbroker, jeweller, and clothier
Nelson, B., 63; Pawnbroker.

LUNCOMBE STREET.

Monet, S.; Draper.

DUNCOMBE STREET.

Monet, S.; Draper.

DURHAM STREET.

Wilson, Jas., 28; Pawnbroker, jeweller, and clothier.

MIDDLESBOROUGH.

Commercial Directory of the Jews of Gt. Britain.

East Street.

Wilkes, M., 25 and 27 ; Clothier and jeweller.

Gilkes Street.

Steinberg, A., 9 ; " The Perseverance Furnishing Co."

Grange Road, W.

Simon, H., 66 ; Financial agent.

Marton Road.

Phillips, N. ; Financial agent.

Milton Street.

Gerstone, J. ; Draper.

Newport Road.

Behrman, D., 189 ; Complete house-furnisher.
Berger, Jos., 179 and 181 ; Boot and shoe dealer.
Bernstein, J., 145; Pawnbroker, jeweller, and clothier.
Levy, J., 151 ; Pawnbroker, jeweller, and clothier.
Smith, J., 104 ; Wholesale and retail clothier.

North Ormesby.

Levy, L., 73 and 75, Smeaton Street, and Cargo Fleet Road, and East Street ; Pawnbroker, jeweller, and clothier.

Peacock Street.

Davis, B. (Rev.) ; Minister Hebrew congregation.

Punch Street.

Reubens, B. ; Slipper manufacturer.

MIDDLESBOROUGH.

Commercial Directory of the Jews of Gt. Britain.

South Street.

Isaacs, G. ; Pawnbroker.
Levy, Jac., 7 ; Clothier and jeweller.

Zetland Road.

Wilks, J. ; Financial agent.

NEWCASTLE-ON-TYNE.

Bath Lane Terrace.

Feldman, L., 33 ; Wholesale and retail slipper manfr.
Freeman, Marks, 25 ; Retail draper.
Meltzer, N. ; Wholesale and retail draper and clothier.
Rose, Chas., 17 ; Wholesale slipper manufacturer.

Beaconsfield Street.

Cohen, Morris, 48 ; General dealer and picture-framer.
Ungar, H., 229 ; Dealer in jewelry, furniture, etc.

Blackett Street.

Goldberg, M., 55 ; Tailor and draper.

Blandford Street.

Abrahams, L., 32 ; Merchant and master tailor.
Block, Wolf, 30 ; Wholesale and retail draper.
Lukes, Jac., 76 ; Merchant tailor and tailor for the trade.
Marks, David, 35 ; Ladies' and gent's clothing.

Blenheim Street.

Cohen, David, 59 ; Wholesale and retail jeweller.
Horowitz Bros., 13 ; Wholesale drapers.

NEWCASTLE-ON-TYNE.

Commercial Directory of the Jews of Gt. Britain.

Campbell Street.

Cohen, Louis S., 34 ; Wholesale and retail jeweller.

Charlotte Square.

Cohen, Isidore, 6½ ; Wholesale slipper manufacturer.

Marcus, S., 6½ ; Wholesale, boot, shoe, and slipper manufacturer and leather merchant.

Clayton Street.

Freedland, Jac., 91 ; Master tailor and tailor for the trade.

Pass, Benj., 78 ; London, Birmingham, and Sheffield goods, and importer glass, china, and fancy ware.

Collingwood Street.

Turner, Sol., 50 ; Financier.

Cromwell Street.

Kenn, M., 78; Wholesale and retail draper and clothier.

Rosenbloom, D., 76 ; Wholesale and retail draper and clothier.

Rosenthal, I., 48 ; Wholesale jeweller.

Day Street.

Joseph, M. T., 16 ; Jeweller.

Gloucester Street.

Rosenberg, Jos., 27 ; Watchmaker and jeweller.

Grainer Street.

Abrahams, G. L., 29 ; Jeweller and silversmith.

NEWCASTLE-ON-TYNE.

Commercial Directory of the Jews of Gt. Britain.

Bernstone, J. H., 13 ; Financial Agent.
London Emporium ; Jewelry and fancy dealers.

Hamilton Street.

Benjamin, Louis, 24 ; Wholesale and retail dealer in watches, gold and silver alberts, etc.
Harris, Sol., 42 ; Merchant tailor and outfitter.

Hartington Street.

Barnard, T., 14 ;. Jeweller and general dealer.

Howard Street.

Barnett, D., 15 ; Wholesale slipper manufacturer.

John Street.

Goldberg, Isaac, 19 ; Wholesale cabinet manufacturer.

Lawton Street.

Mendelssohn, Rev. L., B.A. ; Minister.

Low Friar Street.

Benjamin, M., 22 ; General clothier.

Middlecross Street.

Cohen, Saml., 35 ; Synagogue official restaurant.

Nelson Street.

Cohen, Moses, 4 ; Custom and master tailor.

New Bridge Street.

Harris, R., 52 ; also 105, Northumberland Street ; London and Counties Dental Supply Co.
Myer, G., Hunter's Yard ; Art cabinet manufacturer ; and at 64, Low Friar Street ; broker, and clothier.

NEWCASTLE-ON-TYNE.

Commercial Directory of the Jews of Gt. Britain.

NEWGATE.

Adelstone, L., 95 ; Leather merchant.
Grunthal, J., 47 ; Pawnbroker and jeweller.
Moskow, Saml., 75 ; Darn Crook ; Watchmaker and jeweller.

NORTHUMBERLAND COURT.

Morris, R. ; Wholesale cabinet maker ; sideboard and bedroom suites a specialty.

NORTHUMBERLAND STREET.

Lowe, I., Elswick Court ; Furniture dealer.

NUN STREET.

Schwartz, Henry, 9 ; High-class tailor and tailor for the trade.

PERCY STREET.

Robinson, Parks, 26 ; Slipper and leggings manfr.

PILGRIM STREET.

Falk, D. ; Foreign money exchange and jeweller.
Jacobs, Morris, Forsyth Court ; and at Elswick Court ; Wholesale cabinet manufacturer.

PINK LANE.

Sommerfield and Sons ; Pawnbrokers and jewellers.
Woolf, G. ; Wholesale and retail picture-frame manufacturer and dealer in fine arts.

RICHMOND STREET.

Jenkins, David, 20 ; Wholesale slipper manufacturer.

RIDLEY VILLAS.

Solomon, S., 8. ; Jeweller and general dealer.

NEWCASTLE-ON-TYNE.

Commercial Directory of the Jews of Gt. Britain.

Rye Hill.

Benjamin, I., 15 ; Jeweller and general dealer.

Scotswood Road.

Bernstein, Moses, 295 ; General dealer.
Goodman, Isadore, 348–350 ; Watchmaker, jeweller, and dealer in fancy goods.
Kossick, Louis, 24–26 ; and 17, New Bridge Street ; Carver, gilder, and picture-frame manufacturer.
Vineburg, Julius, 5, Elswick Terrace ; Wholesale boot, shoe, and slipper manufacturer.

Stanhope Street.

Asher, A., 62 ; Jeweller.

Stone Street.

Abelskie, Nathan, 206 ; Jeweller, watchmaker, etc.
Rottersman, D., 79 ; Watchmaker and jeweller.

Sunderland Street.

Richman, Louis, 12 ; Family baker.

Tarset Street, Battlefield.

Fenwick, Myer, 18 ; General draper.

The Quay.

Lotinga ; Shipbroker.

Trafalgar Street.

Levin, Chas., 8 ; Painter and decorator.

Villa Place.

Appelbaum, Rev. Davis, 48 ; Cantor and Mohel.
Jacobs, Frank, 6, High Villa Place ; Master tailor.
Levi, Harris, 50 ; Merchant tailor.

NEWCASTLE-ON-TYNE.

Commercial Directory of the Jews of Gt. Britain.

WESTGATE ROAD.

Library of the Newcastle Beth Hammidrash, 225.
Rose, Louis, 171 ; Tobacconist and fancy goods.
Wiener, Nathan, 179 ; Watchmaker and wholesale and retail dealer in jewelry and fancy goods.

WESTMORLAND STREET.

Mickler, A., & Co., 23 ; Wholesale drapers.

WESTMORLAND TERRACE.

Brown, L., 35 ; Pawnbroker, jeweller, and clothier.
Falk, Michael, 56 ; Wholesale jeweller.

HEATON.

Finn, Moses, 97, Tynemouth Road ; Draper.

BYKER.

Alexander, Saml., 41 ; and at 75, Walker Road, High Walker ; Pawnbroker and clothier.
Marks, A., 33–35, Raby Street ; Picture-frame and hardware dealer.

SHIELDFIELD.

GLADSTONE STREET.

Levy, Nathan, 9 ; Wholesale slipper manufacturer.
Merkel, Chas., 22 ; Wholesale dealer in second-hand watches.

GOSFORTH STREET.

Kossick & Marks, 50–52 ; Pawnbrokers and clothiers

NEWCASTLE-ON-TYNE.

Commercial Directory of the Jews of Gt. Britain.

HENRY STREET.

Levin, A., 40 ; Jeweller.

SHIELD STREET.

Cohen, Ph., 42 ; Wholesale and retail boot, shoe, and slipper manufacturer.
Levy, Saml., 186–188 ; Wholesale boot, shoe, and slipper manufacturer.

SHIELDFIELD GREEN.

Jackson, H., & J., 9 ; Wholesale sewn and rivetted slipper manufacturers.

SHIELDFIELD LANE.

Kinsler, M., 20 ; Wholesale slipper manufacturer.

SIDE.

Van Der Velde & Co., 44 ; Works, 5, Dean Street ; Die sinkers, seal, brass, door, cart, window-plates, and heraldic engravers. Est. 1862.

NEWPORT, MON.

ALEXANDRA ROAD.

Bloom, A. &. E., 3 ; Pawnbrokers.

COMMERCIAL ROAD.

Bloom, S. D., 44 ; Furnishers.
Goldstein, W., 77 ; Pawnbroker and clothier.
Jacobs, A. I. & E., 96, 97, Liverpool House ; Wholesale and retail outfitters.
Jacobs, P., 163 ; Pawnbroker and clothier.
Manoy, M., 35 ; Pawnbroker.

NEWPORT.

Commercial Directory of the Jews of Gt. Britain.

Dock Street.

Freedman, P. & Co., 1–4, Market Buildings ; Cabinet makers, upholsterers, and picture-moulding manufacturers ; also at Swansea and Sheffield.

Hirsch, B., 141 ; Clothier.

Phillips, W., 164 ; Pawnbroker.

High Street.

Isaacson, B., 30 ; Piano and music warehouse.

Tredegar Place.

Abrahamson, L. S., 9 ; Jeweller and pawnbroker ; also at Cardiff and Treforest.

William Street.

Field, B,, 31 ; Jeweller.

Rev. Dr. Berlin ; Minister Hebrew congregation.

NORFOLK.

NORWICH.

Ber Street.

Isaacson, Saml., 71a ; Clothier and custom tailor.

Bethel Street.

Rose & Smith, Blazeby's Yard ; Master tailor.

Briggs' Street.

Fredman, J. ; Silversmith.

Castle Street.

Symons, S., 6 ; Furnisher ; and at Duke's Place ; Flock manufacturer and rag and metal merchant.

NORFOLK.

Commercial Directory of the Jews of Gt. Britain.

FAITH'S LANE.
Schulman, Rev.; Min. Heb. Congregation.

MADDERMARKET.
Brahams, D., 11; Fashionable London tailor.

MARKET PLACE.
Urbinsky, Louis, 19, The Walk; Artist and high-class photographer.

PEACOCK STREET.
Harrison, S. H., 52; Works: North Heigham Mills; Flock manufacturer and rag and metal merchant.

POTTERGATE STREET.
Levine, Louis, 19; Silversmith and Pawnbroker.

QUEEN STREET.
Haldenstein & Son; Boot and shoe manufacturers.

ROSE LANE.
Freeman, W., 57; Military and civil tailor.

ST. ANDREW'S HALL PLAIN.
Leveton, J., Picture-frame manufacturer, &c.

ST. GREGORY'S ALLEY.
Levine, J., 4; Silversmith.

SILVER STREET.
Ecker, Louis, 34; Master tailor.

STACY ROAD.
Herrman, Henry, 24; Boot and shoe manufacturer.

NORFOLK.

Commercial Directory of the Jews of Gt. Britain.

TIMBERHILL STREET.
Samuel, B, ; Pawnbroker, jeweller and clothier.

UPPER GOAT LANE.
Soman & Son ; Printers and puhlishers.

GREAT YARMOUTH.

BLACKFRIARS ROAD.
Bernstein, Jos., 51 ; Bespoke tailor and cutter.

GORLESTON.
Joseph, J. A. ; Merchant.

KING STREET.
Goldstone, Abm., 134 ; Merchant tailor and draper.
Lewis, Mendel, 130 ; Picture-frame maker, &c.

MARKET ROW.
Rosenthal, H., 5 ; Bespoke tailor, hatter, and hosier.

ST. PETER'S ROAD.
Jones, John, 32 ; Lapidary and dealer in fancy goods.

NORTHAMPTON.
Lubetzki, Rev. ; Reader Heb. Cong.

AGNES ROAD.
Kronson ; Boot and shoe agent.

NORTHAMPTON.

Commercial Directory of the Jews of Gt. Britain.

Albert Street.
Geofrey ; Master tailor.

Andrew Street.
Solomon ; Boot and shoe manufacturer.

Bridge Street.
Lyons, Miss ; House-furnisher.

Dunster Street.
Morris ; Master tailor.

Lady's Lane.
Hayman ; Randall's boot and shoe factory.

Newland.
Michel, G. L. ; Leather merchant and importer.
Michel, D. & Co. ; Boot and shoe manufacturers.
Michel, Miss ; Agent Remington type writer.

St. Michael's Mt.
Bernow ; Financial agent.

Turner Street.
Glassman Bros. ; Boot and shoe finishers.

Waterloo.
Michaelson ; Financial Agent.

NORTH SHIELDS.

Church Way.
Cohen ; Pawnbroker and clothier.
Fisher, J. M. ; Pawnbroker and jeweller.

NORTH SHIELDS.

CLIVE STREET.
Merkel, C. D., 50; Pawnbroker and foreign money exchange.
Morris, M., 34; Clothier and jeweller.

RUDYERD STREET.
Freudenberg, A., 18; Picture-frame manufacturer and print dealer.

NOTTINGHAM.

ALBERT STREET.
Herzfeld, M., 7; and 33, Clumber Street; Wholesale and retail cigarette manufr. and tobacconist.

ALFRETON ROAD.
Brener, D., 181; Hosier and small-wares dealer.
Livingstone, L., 33, Mitchell Street; Master tailor.

BARKERGATE.
Braun; Lace Merchant.
Feilman, J. & Co.; Lace merchants.
Fleischheimer; Lace merchant.

BIRKLAND AVENUE.
Cohen, Harris, Rev.; Min. Hebrew Cong.

BRIDLESMITH GATE.
Silverberg, J., 5, Pepper Street; Master tailor.

CARLTON STREET.
Goldman, Ralph, 19; Bespoke London tailor.

NOTTINGHAM.

Commercial Directory of the Jews of Gt. Britain.

CASTLE TERRACE.
Rosenberg, S., 29; Master tailor.

CHESTERFIELD STREET.
Silverston, Em., 13; Wall-paper and general dealer.

COALPIT LANE.
Harbour, A., 47; Manager for Dixon & Co., wholesale clothiers.

DERBY ROAD.
Cahn, A.; Nottingham Furnishing Co.
Harris, I., 9b, Toll Street; Master tailor.
Samuel, J.; Pawnbroker and jeweller.
Simon, Louis, 39; Wholesale and retail wall-paper.

GILL STREET.
Fisher, Leon, 19; Jeweller.

GLASSHOUSE STREET.
Karmel Louis, 26; also Union Road and Sussex Street; Pawnbroker, jeweller and clothier.

GT. ALFRED STREET.
Moses, Robert, 179; Merchant tailor.

HEATHCOTE BUILDINGS.
Koski & Co.; Merchant tailors.

HOCKLEY.
Goldstone, Louis, 8; Wholesale and retail fents.

LONG ROW.
Alexander, Theobald, 40; Clothier and outfitter. Est. 1878.

NOTTINGHAM.

Commercial Directory of the Jews of Gt. Britain.

Market Place.
Boodson, Nathan, 69, Mount Street; Master tailor.

Park Row.
Snapper, David, 43; Draper and wall-paper merchant.

Parkinson Street.
Kaufman, J., 10; Custom tailor.

Parliament Street.
Glassman, Saml., Woodland Place; Master tailor.
Kleyne, E., Byron Bldgs.; Tailor and habit-maker.
Levy, Ph., Cullen's Yard; Master tailor.

Peck Lane.
Block, A. S.; Financier.

Radford.
Fox, Jos., 6, Sullivan Street; Jeweller.

Sneinton Road.
Benedict, S., 10; Pawnbroker and tailor.

Stoney Street.
Heyman, Alexander, and Co.; Lace merchants.
Jacoby and Co.; Lace merchants.
Liepman, Kohn, and Co.; Lace merchants.
Meyer, Paul; Lace merchant.
Stibel, Kaufmann, and Co., Lace merchants.
Wineberg, J.; Lace merchant.

NOTTINGHAM.

Commercial Directory of the Jews of Gt. Britain.

STRATTON STREET.
Rosenblatt, D.; Chamois leather dresser; also 7, Hutchison Street.

UNION ROAD.
Coster, Hyman, 43; Cigar maker.

WATERWAY STREET.
Snapper Sol., 114; Draper.

WEST BRIDGFORD.
Schulman, Wolfe, 10, Rushworth Avenue; Jeweller.

WOODBOROUGH ROAD.
Rabbinowitch, Bros., 120; Jewellers.

OXFORD.

CORN MARKET STREET.
Zacharias, J., & Co., 26, 27; Waterproof manufrs.

KINGSTON ROAD.
Winternitz, Dr., 100; Professor.

NORHAM GARDEN.
Neubauer, Dr., 6; Professor and Librarian.

OXFORD UNIVERSITY.
Sylvester, Dr.; Professor Geometry.

OXFORD.

Commercial Directory of the Jews of Gt. Britain.

St. Clement's.
Crook ; Furnisher.
Davidson, D., 57A ; General dealer.

St. Elbe's.
Davidson, G., 2, Prince's Street ; Jeweller.
Goldstone, I., 6, Church Street ; Jeweller.

St. John Street.
Franks, B. J., 21 ; Dental surgeon.

Synagogue House.
Zacchieni, Rev. J. ; Reader Hebrew congregation.

PLYMOUTH, DEVONPORT.

Athanæum Street.
Samuels, S., 16 ; Financier.

Buckland Street.
Conitz, L., 3 ; General dealer.

Cecil Street.
Brock, L., 67 ; Musician.

Exeter Street.
Abrahams, A. ; Picture-frame maker, etc.
London, H,, 139 ; Pawnbroker and clothier.

Frankfort Street.
Brock, C. ; Watchmaker and jeweller.

PLYMOUTH.

Commercial Directory of the Jews of Gt. Britain.

Brock, J. ; Watchmaker and bicycle dealer.
Cohen, A. ; Pawnbroker and clothier.
Freedman, M. ; House-furnisher.
Jacobs, M., Frankfort House ; Jeweller and rag merchant.

HIGH STREET.

Jacobs, J. ; Jeweller and silversmith.

LAMBEY HILL.

Jacobs, J. ; Fish merchant.

MORLEY STREET.

Bromberg, S., 6 ; General dealer.

OXFORD STREET.

Jacobs, H., 7 ; Jeweller and silversmith.
Spier, A. N., 29 ; Oxford Place ; Ex-Min. Heb. Cong.

ROCKVILLE, MANAMEAD.

Bischofswerder, D. ; Diamond merchant.

RUSSELL STREET.

Plaskowsky, E., 10 ; Furniture dealer.

STONEHOUSE, UNION STREET.

Bischofswerder, 73 ; Jeweller and silversmith.
Brand, T. ; Complete house-furnisher.
Brock, A., 109 ; Jeweller and electroplater.
Lazarus, I., 65 ; Complete house-furnisher.
Orgel, E., 182 ; Furniture manufacturer.
Roseman, I., 30 ; Complete house-furnisher.

PLYMOUTH.

Commercial Directory of the Jews of Gt. Britain.

Tavistock Road.

Conich, A., 21; Tobacconist and importer and domestic cigars.

Treville Street.

Simpson, S., 77; Furniture and portmanteau manufacturer. Branch: Fore Street, Exeter.

Union Street.

Jacobs, J., 177; Furniture manufacturer.
Levy, A., 190; Pawnbroker and Jeweller.
Lewis, M., 155; Picture-frame manufacturer.
Nelson, J., 181; Pawnbroker and antiquarian.

Whimple Street.

Bacsh, E., 18; Antiquarian, etc.

Woolster Street.

Morris, A., 38; Clothier and outfitter.

DEVONPORT.

Catherine Street.

Cohen, J.; Pawnbroker and clothier.
Fredman, L.; House-furnisher, etc.

Fore Street.

Abrahamson, L.; House-furnisher, etc.
Fredman, M., 44; Jeweller and silversmith.

PLYMOUTH.

Commercial Directory of the Jews of Gt. Britain.

MARLBOROUGH STREET.
Cohen, B. ; Dairyman.
Fredman, J., 21 ; House-furnisher, etc.
Joseph, J. ; Clothier and outfitter.
Roseman, M. ; House-furnisher, etc.

ORDNANCE STREET.
Emdon, E., 12 ; Draper and general dealer.

PEMBROKE STREET.
Robins, G. ; House-furnisher, etc.

PORTSEA, PORTSMOUTH.

ALBERT ROAD.
Wolff, Andrew, 90 ; Carver, gilder, and decorator of drawing and dining-rooms in " Carton Pierre." Southsea.

CHURCH PATH.
Burkeman, J., 40 (upper) ; Master tailor of ladies' and gentlemen's trade. Landport. Est. 1887.
Polka, H., 66 ; Master tailor. Landport. Est. 1886.

CLARENCE STREET.
Bernstock, Wolf, 50 ; Master tailor. Landport. Est. 1875.

COLLEGE STREET.
Zeffert, H., & Son, 22 ; Wholesale naval and yachting cap manufacturers. Est. 1860.

PORTSEA.

Commercial Directory of the Jews of Gt. Britain.

COMMERCIAL ROAD.

Franklin, J., 278 and 280 ; Solent furnishing warehouse. Landport. Est. 1887.

COTTAGE GROVE.

Samuel, S. L., & Co., 26 and 43 ; South of England Pianoforte and Furnishing Co. Southsea. Est. 1886.

DORSET STREET.

Sobotki, Isidor, 3 ; Master tailor. Landport. Est. 1885.

ELM GROVE.

Woolfe, Jos. ; Southsea Furnishing Co. Est. 1886.

GOSPORT.

Hart & Co., Gosport House ; Clothiers and outfitters.

HALE STREET.

Bernstein, Isaac, 23 ; Master tailor. Landport. Est. 1887.
Grannard, Abm., 45 ; Master and custom tailor. Landport.

HANOVER STREET.

Edwards, H., 70 ; Tailor and juvenile outfitter.
Jacobs, S., 29 ; Wholesale naval and yachting cap manufacturer.

HIGH STREET.

Abrahams & Son, 93 ; Jewellers.

PORTSEA.

Commercial Directory of the Jews of Gt. Britain.

HYDE PARK ROAD.

Cohen, Morris, 38; Wholesale and retail fruiterer and greengrocer. And at 147, Albert Road, and 38, Church Path, Southsea.

KINGSTON ROAD.

Bernstock, J., 11; Merchant tailor and outfitter. Est. 1875.

LAKE ROAD.

Harris, Newman, 101; Merchant tailor and outfitter. Landport.

Spero, Isaac, 3, Rennie Terrace; Picture-frame manufacturer and picture dealer. Landport. Est. 1883.

MARYLEBONE STREET.

Harris, Abm, 10; Master tailor. Southsea. Est. 1877.

MIDDLE STREET.

Rosen, Mark, 41; Master tailor and habit maker. Southsea.

ORDNANCE ROW.

Emanuel, Alderman A. Leon, Mayor; Consul for Liberia.

Emanuel, H. M., 12 and 13; Jeweller.

Weiner, Marks, 14; Tobacconist. Est. 1887.

PALMERSTON ROAD.

Bobinski, Dr. 1; Dentist. Southsea.

PORTSEA.

Commercial Directory of the Jews of Gt. Britain.

QUEEN STREET.

Levy & Co.; Merchant tailors and outfitters.

Phillips, Rev. I., Synagogue House; Min. and sec. Hebrew congregation.

RUSSELL STREET.

Jacobs & Co., 50; House-furnishers, cabinet makers, upholsterers, and bedding manufacturers. Landport. Factories: 76–78, Sussex Street, Southsea. Est. 1887.

ST. GEORGE'S SQUARE.

Lorie, S. H., Rochester House; Financial agent. Est. in London and Portsea 1849.

Stern, Rev. Dr. Wm.; Prin. Aria College.

SOMERS ROAD, NORTH.

Reubenstein, Lewis, 24; Master tailor. Landport. Est. 1880.

SPRING STREET.

Zeffertt, Lesser, 30; Master tailor. Landport. Est. 1876.

THE HARD.

Emanuel, E. and E., 3; Jewellers to Her Majesty.

UPPER ARUNDEL STREET.

Benjamin, Harris, 34; Master tailor. Landport Est. 1875.

RAMSGATE.

Commercial Directory of the Jews of Gt. Britain.

ALBION ROAD.
Van Praagh, Mrs. B., 6 ; Private.

ARKLOW TERRACE.
Barnett, B., 4 ; Private.

AUGUSTA ROAD.
Barnett, Mrs., 7 ; Boarding-house.
Da Costa, A., 10 ; Boarding-house.
Twyman, The Misses, 17 ; Boarding-house.

EAST CLIFF.
Montefiore, J. Sebag ; East Cliff Lodge.

GRANVILLE TERRACE.
Isaac, Mrs , 6 ; Private.

HARBOUR STREET.
Cohen, J., 23 ; Hairdresser and perfumer.
Cohen, S. H. ; Hairdresser and perfumer.
Hart, L., 7 ; China and glass dealer.

HÉRESON.
Brave, Mrs. de, 2, Florry Cottage ; Private.
Cohen, The Misses, 1, Florry Cottage ; Private.
Harris, Mrs., 3, Florry Cottage ; Private.
Tritsch, J., Hereson House ; Secretary of Synagogue and College.
White, W., White Villa ; Private.

RAMSGATE.

Commercial Directory of the Jews of Gt. Britain.

Judith Montefiore College.
Hirschfield. Dr. H., 2 ; Professor of College.
Schewzig, Dr. B., 8 ; Professor of College.

King Street.
Barnett, J., 37 ; House-furnisher.
Barnett, S., 49 ; Hairdresser and perfumer.
Da Costa, J., 66 ; Clothier.
Jones, J., 108 ; General dealer.
Lazarus, S., 75 ; Pawnbroker and clothier.

Mill House.
Shandel, H. (Rev.) ; Reader Heb. congregation.

Shaftsbury Street.
Afriga, S., 9 ; Boarding-house.

Temple Cottage.
Belasco, G. (Rev.) ; Min. Heb. congregation.

Thanet Road.
Caro, Mrs., 4 ; Private.

Townley Castle.
Harris, S. H. (Rev.) ; Prin. Townley Castle College.

Victoria Parade.
Solomon, The Misses, 3 ; Boarding-house.

York Terrace.
Abrahams, J., 11 ; Boarding-house.

READING.

Commercial Directory of the Jews of Gt. Britain.

Blagrave Street.

Fooks, S., 37 ; Ladies' tailor, costumier, and habit maker.

Chatham Street.

Ehrenberg, I., 120 ; and at 34, Battle Street ; Gentlemen's bespoke clothing manufacturer.

Cross Street.

Goldman, I. ; Merchant tailor.

Foundry Street.

Myers, Isaac, 17 ; Master and custom tailor.

Oxford Road.

Bernstein, M., 243 ; Financial agent.

Queen's Road.

Solomon, Harris, 20, Queen's Crescent ; Ladies' and gentlemen's custom and master tailor.

Tencer, S., 98 ; Tailor.

Somer's Town.

Cohen, A., 40 ; Tailor.

Upper Crown Street.

Cohen, Hyman, 23 ; Master and custom tailor.

SHEFFIELD.

Commercial Directory of the Jews of Gt. Britain.

CUMBERLAND STREET.

Agar, Maurice H., Hollandshire Works, Branch 30, Wicker; Wall-paper manufacturer and general dealer. And at Harcourt Place, Scarboro'.

ECCLESALL ROAD.

Newman & Samuels, 50; Practical bespoke tailoring establishment.

HIGH STREET.

Kaminski, Edward, 5; Auctioneer, valuer, and commission agent.

MARKET STREET.

Brown, H. L., 71; Watch manufacturer and jeweller.

NORFOLK STREET.

Baum, M., 193; Electro silver-plate manufacturer.

SNIG HILL.

Finestone, Davis, 68; and 268, Shalesmoor; House furnisher, cabinet maker, and general merchant.

UNION STREET.

Neumann, M., 17; Wholesale and retail glass merchant.

SHEFFIELD.

Commercial Directory of the Jews of Gt. Britain.

West Bar.

Neumann, J., 92–93; Wholesale and retail lead and glass merchant.

Waters, L., 19; Branch: 45, South Street; Fashionable clothier and outfitter.

West Bar Green.

Jacobs, Michael, 51; Financial agent.

Rootsten, Lewis, 40; Wholesale picture-frame and moulding manufacturer.

Wicker.

Isaacs, Lewis, 90-92; Wholesale and retail paper-hanging merchant. Est. 1868.

SOUTH SHIELDS, DURHAM.

Adelaide Street.

Pearlman, Isaac, 121–3; Pawnbroker, clothier, and jeweller.

Cuthbert Street.

Marks, Henry, 27; Watchmaker and jeweller.

Dean Street.

Cohen, I., & Son; and at Thrift Street; Clothiers, jewellers, and opticians.

SOUTH SHIELDS.

Commercial Directory of the Jews of Gt. Britain.

Derby Street.

Jackson, Henry, cor. Derby and Cuthbert Streets ; Antique furniture dealer.

Frederick Street.

Dreebin, L., 123 ; The Lansdale Coal Supply Co.

Green Street.

Alprovich, Harris, 24 ; Pawnbroker and jeweller.
Josephs, D., 19 ; Boot and shoe dealer.
Josephs, L., 33-34 ; Boot and shoe dealer.

Mile End Road.

Gompertz, S., 59 ; Pawnbroker and clothier.

Saville Street.

Cohen, Chas., 40 ; Drapery and furniture dealer.
Pearlman, Jos., 6 ; Coal merchant.

Thrift Street.

Gompertz, Aaron S., 22 ; Pawnbroker and jeweller.
Levy, Sol., 1 ; and 95, E. Holborn ; Pawnbroker.

Ocean Road.

Finn, Samuel, 50 ; Tailor and draper.

SOUTHAMPTON.

Commercial Directory of the Jews of Gt. Britain.

ALBION PLACE.

Emanuel, A. ; Solicitor.
Emanuel & Emanuel, 14 ; Solicitors.

ANGLESEA PLACE.

Silverman, S. M. ; Furnishing emporium.

BEVIS VALLEY.

Cohen, M. ; Pawnbroker and furnisher.

BRIDGE ROAD.

Franks, J., 12 ; Tailor,
Hart, J. (street) ; Domestic bazaar.
Hyams, A., 36 ; Tailor.
Hyams, J., 18 ; Tailor.
Levy, N. (street), 21 ; Clothier.
Van Praag (street), 11 ; Watchmaker and jeweller.

CANUTE ROAD.

Gerth, R. A. ; Bureau de change.

CUMBERLAND PLACE.

Emanuel, S. M., J. P., 19 ; Retired.

FRENCH STREET.

Cohen, Mrs. N., 24 ; Pawnbroker and clothier.

HIGH STREET.

Emanuel, M., J. P. ; Pawnbroker and jeweller.

SOUTHAMPTON.

Commercial Directory of the Jews of Gt. Britain.

MARLAND PLACE.
Phillips, M., 83 ; Retired.

NEWTOWN.
Levene, L., 2, Cranbury Terrace ; Auctioneer and valuer.

ORCHARD STREET.
Solomon, M., 37 ; General dealer.

OXFORD STREET.
Arbus, S. ; Hairdresser and perfumer.
Jacobs, S. A. ; Manager London and Provincial Furnishing Co.

PORTLAND STREET.
Cohen, L., 7 ; Financier.

ST. MARY'S ROAD.
Fyne, Rev. S. ; Minister Hebrew congregation.

ST. MARY'S STREET.
Harris, Mrs. N., 40 ; Clothier and outfitter.
Herman, D., 137 ; Hairdresser and perfumer.
Kaplan, J., 12 ; Fish and oil dealer.

SHIRLEY STREET.
Moses, M. A., 143 ; Fruiterer.

VICTORIA STREET.
Corbett, J. ; Painter and decorator.   Woolston.

SOUTHPORT.—Lancs.

Commercial Directory of the Jews of Gt. Britain.

ALBERT ROAD.
Harris, Dr. F., 13. Oculist.

ARBOUR STREET.
Tumin, S., 41. Manchester merchant.

ASH STREET.
Blumberg. Manchester merchant.

ASHLEY ROAD.
Broudy & Cohen, 11. General Furnishing Co., Drapers and clothiers.

KENSINGTON ROAD.
Hompies, J., 99. Cigar Manufacturer.

KNOWSLEY ROAD.
Lambert, Mrs. J., Sorrento. Orthodox Jewish Boarding House.
Harris, S. M., Sorrento. Antiques merchant.

LONDON STREET.
Price, H. & Son. Complete house-furnishers.

MAPLE STREET.
Markusfield, 14. General dealer.

OAK STREET.
Moss, Lionel, 36. Manchester merchant.

PARK CRESENT.
Levi, A. de. The Grange. Manchester merchant.

SOUTHPORT.

Commercial Directory of the Jews of Gt. Britain.

Levi, E. R. de, The Grange. Manchester merchant

PROMENADE.

Besso, A., 70. Manchester merchant

SCARISBRICK ROAD.

Finkelstine, H., 20. Complete house-furnisher.
Levy, Rev. N., (retired).
Levy, Sol., Traveler.

SHAKESPEARE STREET.

Dannenberg, S., Complete house-furnisher.
Kauffman, N., Cabinet manufacturer.
Liverman, Jacob, 2, Bentham st. Family grocer and provision dealer.

SUSSEX ROAD.

Loewy, J. J., see Bradford.

TULKETH STREET.

Edelston, General dealer.

STOCKPORT, CHESHIRE.

Commercial Directory of the Jews of Gt. Britain.

Brinksway.
Berman, Benj., 9, Albert Street ; Master tailor.

Chestergate.
Bernstein, Reuben, 197 ; Master tailor.
Finkelstein, S. ; Draper.
Franks, Isaac, 9, Swain Street ; Master tailor.

Dow Bank.
Bernstein, B., 30, Swain Street ; Master tailor.
Schwarzberg, P., 32 ; Clothier.

Heaton Lane.
Cohen, Marcus, 25, Hatton Street ; Master tailor.
Morris ; Grocer.
Tarshish ; Furniture dealer.

Heaton Norris.
Freedman, S., 138, Love Lane ; Merchant tailor.

Hillgate.
Bowman, David, 7 (higher), Hindley Street ; Master tailor.
Livermann, Louis, 1 (middle) ; House-furnisher.
Winter, J., 25, Little Underbank ; Watchmaker, &c.

Lord Street.
Rubenson ; Master tailor.

Queen Street.
Isaacs, Sol. ; Master tailor.
Platt, Saml., 16 ; Master tailor.

STOCKPORT.

Commercial Directory of the Jews of Gt. Britain.

Steinman, R. Rev. ; Reader and teacher.
Zaklan, L., 38 ; Custom tailor.

WOOD STREET.

Bernstein, H. ; Tailor.
Levein, Simon, 9 ; Master tailor.
Moses, I. ; Tailor.

STOCKTON, DURHAM.

Bernstein, P. ; Pawnbroker.
Bloom, A. ; Pawnbroker.
Brewer ; Draper.
Cohen ; Financial agent.
Goetz, Clothier.
Goldstone ; Pictures.
Hyams ; Pawnbroker.
Lenrman ; Draper.
Michelson ; Pawnbroker.
Myers ; Pawnbroker.
Shulman ; Draper.

DARLINGTON.

Gilbert, S. ; General dealer.
Gordon, S. Rev.
Honigbaum, J. ; Smallware.
Hyams, S. ; Travelling jeweller.
Levy, S. ; Draper.

STOCKTON.

Commercial Directory of the Jews of Gt. Britain.

Richardson, J. ; Financial agent.
Schott, J., 1, Granville Terrace ; Financial agent.
Sluifko, E., 6, Duke Street ; Draper and general dealer.
Stone, J. ; Draper.

STROUD, GLOSTER.

Acre Street.

Levy, Isaac, 30 ; Master tailor.

Horn's Road.

Whitehead, Marcus, 2, Cobden Villas ; Master tailor.

John Street.

Sperber, S. ; House-furnisher, upholsterer, and exporter of mouldings, engravings, &c.

King Street.

Shane, I. Minden ; Master tailor.

Landsdown Hill.

Greensweig, E., Lock & Hill Villa ; Master Tailor.
Levy, Marks, Lock and Hill Villa ; Master tailor.
Malinski, Morris ; Master tailor.

Nelson Street.

Levy, Lewis, Farr's Lane ; Master tailor and provision dealer.

STROUD.

Commercial Directory of the Jews of Gt. Britain.

Slad Road.

Berman Chas. ; Master tailor and provision dealer.
Englishmann, Isaac ; Licensed victualler and master tailor.
Goldstein, Jos,, 105 ; Master tailor.
Levy, Hyman, 106 ; Master tailor.
Rosenberg, A. Rev., 23, Springfield Terrace ; Min. Heb. Congregation.

Whitehall.

Greensweig, I. ; Master tailor.

SUNDERLAND.

Alexandra Terrace.

Goldman, Chas., 21 ; Pawnbroker and clothier.

Ann Street.

Kantrowitz, Rev. ; Reader Heb. congregation.
Levy, H., 16 ; Teacher and collector.
Levy, Jos., 16 ; Sec. Heb. congregation and Board of Guardians.
Phillips, J. (Rev.) ; Minister Heb. congregation.

Borough Road.

Friedman, Asher, 8 ; Draper and general dealer.

Church Street.

Cohen, M., & Co., 15 ; and 182, High Street, E. Pawnbrokers, jewellers, and clothiers.

SUNDERLAND.

Commercial Directory of the Jews of Gt. Britain.

CLEMENTINA STREET.
Moses, Moses, 1 ; General dealer.

CORONATION STREET.
Friedman, B., 86 ; Wholesale and retail ladies' and children's ware.

COUSIN STREET, HENDON.
Olswang, D. A., 31 ; Furnisher, jeweller, etc.

DURHAM STREET, S.
Berman, J., 50 ; Hat and cap manufacturer.

FORE STREET.
Harris, Lewis, 19 ; Pawnbroker and general dealer.

FOYLE STREET.
Cohen, Myer, 16 ; Bill discounter.

FREDERIC STREET.
Fryde, Emanuel, 40 ; Wholesale and retail jeweller.
Jackson, Elias A., 46 ; Jeweller and general dealer.

HARROWGATE STREET.
Gallowski, G., 59 ; Jeweller and general merchant.
Harris, Israel, 41 ; General dealer.

HEDWORTH TERRACE.
Jacobs, John, & Son, 21 ; Jewellers and drapers.
Lazarus, Jac., 19 ; General dealer.
Morris, David R., 9 ; Jeweller.

SUNDERLAND.

Commercial Directory of the Jews of Gt. Britain.

High Street.

Albert, Harry, 166 ; Hardware merchant.
Berger, E., 158 ; Pawnbroker and money exchange.
Goldberg, Jac., 179 (East) ; Pawnbroker, clothier, and jeweller.
Jacobs, H., 11 ; Wholesale and retail boot, shoe, and slipper manufacturer.
Jacobs, Julius, 187 and 32 (East) : Clothier, jeweller, and foreign money exchange.
Richardson, Newman, 96 (East) ; Pawnbroker and general dealer.
Rothfield & Co., 147 ; Picture-frame manufacturers.

Hudson Road.

Friedman, J., 33 ; Wholesale and retail picture-frame maker.
Jacobs, H., 4 ; Complete house-furnisher.

Lawrence Street.

Gillis, Chas., 7 ; Jeweller and draper.

Manor Place.

Asher, Edward A., 2 ; Jeweller.

Milburn Terrace.

Jacabs, Isaac ; Pawnbroker and general dealer.

Mowbray Terrace.

Gallewski, Ph., 3 ; General house-furnisher.

SUNDERLAND.

Commercial Directory of the Jews of Gt. Britain.

NICHOLSON STREET.
Jacobs, Israel, 11 ; Watchmaker and jeweller.

NILE STREET.
Barclay, I., 32 ; Dealer in fine arts.
Glodt, A., 1 ; Master tailor.
Joseph, Nissan, 51 ; Engraver and lithograper.

NOBLE'S BANK ROAD.
Bergson, Moses ; Jeweller and general dealer.

NORFOLK STREET.
Behrman, Saml., 39 ; General dealer.
Gallewski, Simon, 40 ; Wholesale and general dealer.
Goldman, Isaac, 16 ; Pawnbroker and jeweller.

PARK PLACE, W.
Joseph, M., 2 ; Diamond merchant.

RANDOLPH STREET.
Lewis, Harris, 27 ; Master tailor.

SOUTH STREET.
Joseph, B., 29 ; Saddler and harness maker.

THOMPSON STREET.
Share, A., 7 ; Jeweller and general dealer.

VILLIERS STREET.
Jacoby, G., 33 ; Jeweller.
Shergei, Nathan, 16 ; Clothier and general dealer.

WEAR STREET, HENDON.
Levy, Isaac, 75 ; General dealer.

SUNDERLAND.

Commercial Directory of the Jews of Gt. Britain.

West Sunniside.
Wolfe, A., 29 ; Bill discounter and watchmaker.

Winifred Terrace.
Friedman, Moses, 3 ; Jeweller.

WIGAN.

Darlington Street.
Ableson, Chas., 37 ; and at Bolton ; Furnisher and upholsterer.
Marks, M., 57 ; Wholesale and retail smallware and hardware dealer.

Manchester Road, Ince.
Niman, Isadore, 184 ; Tailor and draper.

School Lane.
Niman & Sytner, 32 ; Tailors for the trade.

Standishgate.
Kresner, A., 124 ; Tailor and draper.

WOLVERHAMPTON.

Chapel Ash.
Webber, I., Jubilee House ; Boot maker.

Railway Street.
Beaver, S., 3 ; Master tailor.
Schwerin, 2 ; Draper and general dealer.

WOLVERHAMPTON.

Commercial Directory of the Jews of Gt. Britain.

Queen Street.

Benjamin, L. ; Merchant tailor.

St. James' Square.

Aarons, Rev. ; Teacher.
Hart, J. ; Financier.
Levy, I. (Rev.), 13 ; Reader.
Morris, B., 6 ; Picture-frame maker.
Tumpowsky, D., 8 ; Jeweller and general dealer.

Salop Street.

Barnet, M. ; Furnisher and clothier.
Goldenberg, M., 123 ; Glass dealer.
Goldstone, H., 86 ; Furniture and general dealer.
Phillip, J., 15 ; General dealer.

School Street.

Barnet, S. ; Financier.

Snow Hill.

Greenstone, Geo., 43 ; Glass and wall-paper merchant, house painter, and decorator.

Sweetman Street.

Zusman, Z., 213 ; Jeweller.

Tettenhall Road.

Rudelsheim, Z., 99A ; Jeweller.

Waterloo Road.

Harris, J., 17 ; Jeweller.

YORK.
Commercial Directory of the Jews of Gt. Britain.

FRANCES STREET.
Arnoff, S., 38 ; Tailor.
Morris, Sol., 83 ; Master Tailor.
Steinberg, M., 83 ; Tailor.

MONKGATE.
Barnett, M., 54 ; Master tailor.
Solk, H., 54 ; Tailor.

DENNIS STREET, WALMGATE.
Eker, M. (Rev.), 11 ; Reader Hebrew congregation.
Kleinman, S., 14 ; Master tailor.
Solkoff, H., 15 ; Master tailor.

LOWTHER STREET, GROVES.
Israel, Jac., 26 ; Master tailor.
Meddintz, A., 26 ; Tailor.

GILLYGATE.
Rudolph, John, The Terrace ; Financial agent.

IRELAND.

BELFAST.

Commercial Directory of the Jews of Ireland.

BEDEQUE STREET.

Faberlan, Aaron, 30 ; General draper and tailor for the trade.

Jacobson, S., 28 ; General dealer and tailor for the trade.

BEDFORD STREET.

Boas, H., & Co. ; Fancy box manufacturers.

BERRY STREET.

Solomon, F. ; The Ulster Tobacco Co., Ltd.

CROMAC STREET.

Sipiro, I., 143 ; The Cromac delf, china, and hardware dealer.

CULLINGTREE ROAD.

Edelstein, M., 147 ; General draper and house-furnisher. Est. 1884.

DIVIS STREET.

Goldring, J., 87 ; Wholesale and retail draper. Also at 40, Donegall Street, J. & M. ; Financial agents.

Hirson, Harris, 19 ; Draper, furniture dealer, outfitter, etc. Est. 1884.

BELFAST.

Commercial Directory of the Jews of Ireland.

DONEGALL PASS.

Miller, Saml., 120 ; Draper and general dealer.

Sergai, H., 120 ; Dealer in drapery, clocks, looking-glasses, etc.

DONEGALL SQUARE.

Jaffe Bros., 10 ; Linen merchants.

Jaffe Bros, & Co., 5 ; Linen yarn merchants.

FOUNTAIN STREET.

Betzold, George, & Co. ; Linen merchants.

GRESHAM STREET.

Cohen, Jacob, 18 and 28 ; Picture-frame and show-card manufacturer, lithographs and oleographs, etc. And at 41, Smithfield. Est. 1883.

MILL STREET.

Lowenberg, D., 18 ; Watchmaker and silversmith.

NEW KING STREET.

Bogen, I., 24 ; Wholesale picture frame manufacturer, etc. Est. 1881.

OLD LODGE ROAD.

Kochanski, Leon, 6, Conlig Street ; Draper and general dealer.

Rosenfield, Jos., 202 ; Baker, grocer, and provision dealer.

BELFAST.

Commercial Directory of the Jews of Ireland.

SHANKHILL ROAD.

Appleton, Jac., 23, Cumberland Street; Clothier, draper, and general house-furnisher.

Appleton, Ph., 19, Perth Street; Draper and general dealer.

Wolfson, S., 28, Crosbey Street; Draper and general dealer.

VENTRY STREET.

Yochel, Jos., 13; House-furnisher and draper. Est. 1887.

YORK STREET.

Miller, E., 78; Draper, house-furnisher, hardware, and general dealer. Est. 1883.

CORK.

ALBERT STREET.

Clein, L. S., 4, Monrea Terrace; Wholesale draper, furnisher, and boot dealer. Est. 1882.

Elyan, Meyer, 9, Monrea Terrace; General draper and jeweller. Est. 1881.

Sayers, G., 8, Monrea Terrace; General dealer. Est. 1883.

BRIDGE STREET AND CANDEL PLACE.

Spiro, S.; The Standard Watch and Clock Co.; Manufacturers and importers wholesale and retail jewellers.

DOUGLAS STREET.

Jackson, E. L., & Co., 93; Wholesale and retail picture-frame manufacturers and general drapers. Est. 1883.

CORK.

Commercial Directory of the Jews of Ireland.

GREAT GEORGE'S STREET.

Clein, L. S., 49; The Leinster Warehouse Co.; Drapers, outfitters, silk and boot merchants.

HIBERNIAN BUILDINGS.

Jackson, Hy., 44; Draper and general dealer. Est. 1885.

MARINA TERRACE.

Clein, Sol., 9; Wholesale and retail draper and furnisher, etc. Est. 1882.

Glasser, Lewis, 2; Wholesale and retail draper, furnisher, etc. Est. 1883.

Jackson, W., 11; Wholesale and retail draper and general dealer. Est. 1880.

Levin, Aaron, 16; Draper and general dealer. Est. 1885.

NORTH MAIN STREET.

Sayers, N., 10, 11; Complete house-furnisher.

OLD GEORGE'S STREET.

Edelstein, A. M., 30; Wholesale and retail picture-frame manufacturer.

ROCKBORO' ROAD.

Myers, Rev. J. E.; Min. and Sec. Cork Hebrew congregation.

UNIVERSITY.

Hartog; Prof. Cork University.

CORK.

Commercial Directory of the Jews of Ireland.

VICTORIA ROAD.

Abrahamson, I., 7, Elizabeth Terrace ; Draper and general dealer.
Bremsen, D., 4, East Villa ; Draper and general dealer. Est. 1884.
Clein, L., 2, Montenotte View ; Wholesale and retail draper and general agent. Est. 1882.
Clein, Lewis, 2, Elizabeth Terrace ; Draper and general dealer.
Goldberg, S., 8, East Villa ; Draper and general dealer.
Jackson, I., 12, East Villa ; Draper and general dealer. Est. 1884.
Jalkinowitz, J., 6, Elizabeth Terrace ; Draper and general dealer.
Kriger, Sol., 9, Elizabeth Terrace ; Wholesale and retail draper and general dealer.
Rosenthal, I., 6, East Villa ; Draper and general dealer.

Hebrew Benefit Society, Bikur Cholim.
The Rev. Mr. J. E. Myers, Hon. Secretary ; Mr. I. Abrahamson, Treasurer.

DUBLIN.

ASTON QUAY.

Marks., Mrs. Em. E., 1 ; Purchaser and dealer in ladies' and gentlemen's clothing, and naval and military uniforms, jewelry, and antiques. Est. 1859.

DUBLIN.

Commercial Directory of the Jews of Ireland.

Aungier Street.

Levitt Bros., 15 ; General house-furnishers, upholsterers, and carpet warehousemen.

Bray.

Leman, L., 2, Cassandra Villas ; Merchant.

Dame Street.

Isaacs, J., 30 ; Clothier and outfitter.

Dawson Street.

Wexler & Goodman, 33 ; General Supply Co. ; Importers of domestic implements and jewellers.

Fleet Street.

Solomon, Julius, 4 ; Financier and bill broker.

Grafton Street.

Falk, Michael, 32 ; Dealer in silver and articles of vertu.

Reis, Chas. L., & Co., 115 ; Importers jewelry and fancy goods.

Great Brunswick Street.

Goodman, J., 51 ; Banker and bill broker.

Kildare Street.

Laurie, Mdme., 42 ; Clothier and costumier.

Leeson Park.

Van Raath, S. P., 3, Sallymount Terrace ; Teacher Dublin Hebrew congregation.

DUBLIN.

Commercial Directory of the Jews of Ireland.

LOWER CAMDEN STREET.

Burack, R. C., 46 ; Wholesale and retail picture-frame maker and tobacconist.

Jackson, H., & Co., 24 ; General house-furnishers.

Jackson, M., 52 ; Draper and general dealer.

LOWER CLANBRASSEL STREET.

Miller, S., 18 ; Wholesale picture-frame manufacturer and draper.

Noyk, Isaac, 88 ; Wholesale draper, clothier, and boot dealer.

Rozanofsky, W., 89 ; Family grocer, baker, and provision dealer.

Rubin, S., 98 ; Dealer in furniture, drapery, and antiques.

LOWER GARDINER STREET.

Albon, L., 76 ; Watchmaker and jeweller.

Groot, M. de, J. P., 48 ; Merchant. Est. 1852.

LOWER SACKVILLE STREET.

Davies, Messrs., 10 ; Surgeon dentists.

MARY STREET.

Goldberg, M., 57 ; Wholesale drapery and furniture warehouse.

MERRION SQUARE.

Cohen, A., 34, Holles Street ; Clothier and Parisian costumier. Est. 1882.

DUBLIN.

Commercial Directory of the Jews of Ireland.

Nassau Street.

Harris, Morris, 30; Jeweller and dealer in works of art. Est. 1858.

Solomons, M. E., J. P., 19; Optician.

Parliament Street.

Cohen & Myers, 11; The City Furnishing Co.

Diamond, A. B., 5; The Diamond Tobacco Stores; Wholesale and retail tobacconist.

Portobello Road.

Goldberg, S., 19; Draper and general dealer.

Zauberblatt, M., 21; Draper and general dealer.

Rathmines.

Briscoe, Hy., 19, Mt. Pleasant Square; Wholesale and retail draper, clothier, and boot dealer.

Raymond Street.

Kaitcer, H., 55; Commission merchant.

St. Andrew Street.

Harris, Alderman A. W. *(London)*, represented by E. Harris, LL.D., solicitor.

South Circular Road.

Clarke, M., 77, Lombard Street, W.; Wholesale and retail draper.

Cohen, Aaron, 2, Vincent Street; Draper, house-furnisher, etc.

DUBLIN.

Commercial Directory of the Jews of Ireland.

Cohen, B., 2, Vincent Street; Draper, furniture dealer, etc.

Cornick, Winstock & Co., 53, Lombard Street, W.; Wholesale drapers, outfitters, and boot merchants. Est. 1884.

Cristol, David, 1, Walworth Road; Jeweller.

Eliassoff, Elias, 9, Walworth Road; Draper and general dealer.

Glasser, Bernhard, 40, Martin Street; General draper, jeweller, and furniture dealer.

Glasser, N. M., 23, Warren Street; General draper and outfitter.

Golding, Lazarus, 29, Lombard Street, W. Draper and general dealer.

Goldwater, K., 15, Arnott Street; Draper and general dealer.

Greenberg, Jac., 58, Lombard Street, W.; Dealer in Kosher wines. Special wines for Passover.

Greenfield, R., 75, Lombard Street, W.; Jeweller.

Grinspon, M., 1A, Lennox Street; Family grocer, baker, and provision dealer.

Harmel, Michel, 57, Lombard Street, W.; Wholesale draper, outfitter, and boot merchant.

Hirschowitz, Ph., 6, Desmond Street; General dealer and house-furnisher.

Isaacson, L., 23, Lombard Street, W.; General dealer.

Isaacson, S., 30, Lombard Street, W.; Wholesale draper.

Jackson, A. H., 40, Warren Street; Draper and general dealer.

Jackson, J. H., 6, Warren Street; Draper and general dealer.

DUBLIN.

Commercial Directory of the Jews of Ireland.

Jackson, S., 22, Martin Street; Draper and general dealer.

Jackson, Z., 18, Synge Street; Wholesale draper. Est. 1886.

Kadish, H., 6, Desmond Street; General draper and house-furnisher.

Leventon, Rev. Israel; Min. and sec. Heb. cong.

Leventen, Sol., 7, Greenville Avenue; Draper, house-furnisher, and jeweller.

Rubin, Abm., 24, Warren Street; Wholesale and retail watchmaker and jeweller. And at 8, Wexford Street.

Rubin, J. S., 32, Lennox Street; Wholesale and retail draper, outfitter, and boot dealer. Est. 1888.

Shmulowitz, Israel, 15, Vincent Street; Draper and general dealer.

Wachmann, E., 25, Victoria Street; General draper and coal and coke merchant.

Weiner, Henry, 33, Martin Street; Draper and general dealer.

Weiner, I. M., 8, Walworth Road; Draper and house-furnisher.

Weiner, M., 9, Walworth Road; Draper and general dealer.

SOUTH FREDERICK STREET.

Levenston, P.M., R.I.A.M., 35; Mus. Prof.

SUFFOLK STREET.

Rosenthal, J.D., LL.D.; Barrister.

DUBLIN.

Commercial Directory of the Jews of Ireland.

Talbot Street.
Albon, L., 20 ; Watchmaker and jeweller.
Weiner, H., & Co., 33 ; Complete house-furnishers. Branch : 51, Thomas Street.

Trinity Street.
Levitt, Nathan, 6 ; Financial agent and bill broker.

Wellington Quay.
Figatner, Aaron, 26; Ring maker and diamond setter to the trade ; Dealer in precious stones. Est. 1872.
Levenston, Jos., 36 ; Prof. music. Instrumental music academy. Engagements for weddings, etc.

Wicklow Street.
Rosenberg, L., 12 ; Ostrich feather dresser and straw hat maker. Est. 1873.

LIMERICK.

Colooney Street.
Farber, Ephraim, 41 ; Draper and general dealer. Est. 1889.
Goldberg, B., 9 ; Draper and general dealer. Est. 1888.
Goldberg, L., 48 ; General draper, grocer, and provision dealer. Est. 1887.
Graff, Ginsberg & Co., 31 ; Wholesale drapers, clothiers, and boot dealers.

Emmett Place.
Hershblond, M. J., 14 ; Draper and general dealer.
Sless, Jacob, 11 ; Wholesale and retail draper and general dealer. Est. 1888.

George Street.
Davies, Messrs. ; Surgeon dentists.

LIMERICK.

Commercial Directory of the Jews of Ireland.

Mt. Pleasant Avenue.
Keane, M., 15; Draper and general dealer. Est. 1885.

Westland Street.
Greenfield, Benj., 1; Draper and general dealer. Est. 1883.
William-Stein, M., & Co., 25; Drapers, house-furnishers, and general dealers. Est. 1886.

Windmill Street.
Barron, Jac., 2; Wholesale and retail draper, clothier, etc. Est. 1880.

LONDONDERRY.
Myers, Yule, 8, Victoria Terrace, Artillery Street; House-furnisher and draper. Est. 1887.
Robinson, B.; Draper and general house-furnisher.

WATERFORD.

John Street.
Goldring, J. W., 8; House-furnisher and draper.

Johnstown.
Robinson, B., 65; Draper and general house-furnisher.

Manor Street.
Diamond, Louis S., 48; General draper and house-furnisher. Est. 1887.
Smullian, Raphael, 72; General draper and house-furnisher.
Smullian, W., 72; Draper and general dealer.
Toohey, Marcus, 42; Draper and general dealer.

SCOTLAND.

ABERDEEN.

Commercial Directory of the Jews of Gt. Britain.

BROAD STREET.
Geershon, A., 87; Fancy goods merchant.
Geershon, Thos., 57; Clothier and outfitter.

CARMELITE STREET.
Silberzweig, S., 15; General dealer.
Silverman, I., 15; General dealer.

EAST NORTH STREET.
Barnet, I., 44; Picture-frame manufacturer.

GEORGE STREET.
Saltman, I., 394; Waterproof garment manufacturer.

MARISCHAEL STREET.
Littman, Rev. J., 34; Reader Hebrew congregation.

MARKET STREET.
Zarnek, Alex., 48; Financial agent.

NETHER KIRKGATE.
Goodstone, D., 46; General dealer.

QUEEN STREET.
Silverman, A., 38; Boot warehouse.

ABERDEEN.

Commercial Directory of the Jews of Gt. Britain.

Spring Garden.
Bloom, A., 53 ; Slipper manufacturer.

Trinity Quay.
Bittner, Mrs., and Sons, 3 ; Baltie boot warehouse.

EDINBURGH.

Adam Street, E.
Alexander, Myer, 13 ; Jeweller.
Levitus, S., 13 ; Jeweller.

Blackwood Crescent.
Camberg, B., 28 ; Watchmaker and jeweller.

Bristo Street.
Levy, M., 70 ; Wholesale and retail picture-frame manufacturer and glass merchant.
Rosenheim, B., 18 ; Jeweller and general dealer.
Solomon, Henry, 3 (place) ; Tailor. Est. 1856.
Solomon, Wm., 3 (place) ; Watchmaker and jeweller.
Solomon, Mrs. H., 3 (place) ; Boarding.

Buccleugh Street.
Goldberg, P. & B., 14 ; Watchmakers, jewellers, and picture-frame manufacturers.

Caledonian Road.
Levenson, Ph., 10 ; Master tailor and clothier.

Clerk Street.
Rosenberg, J., 1 ; Jeweller.

EDINBURGH.

Commercial Directory of the Jews of Gt. Britain.

CORNWALL STREET.
Lipetz, M., 10 ; Jeweller and watch dealer.

CROSSCAUSEWAY.
Hyman, Isaac, 76 (E.) ; Glazier and glass merchant.
Levinson, M., 5 (W.) ; Jeweller.
Levy, Marcus, 5 (W.) ; Jeweller and watchmaker.
Shirwinter, Jac., 28 (W.) ; Watchmaker and jeweller.
Wasserzug, M., 21 (E.) ; Wholesale and retail jeweller and watchmaker. Est. 1866.

DALKEITH ROAD.
Shirwinter, Julius, 12 ; Jeweller and watchmaker.

DRUMMOND STREET.
Lipetz, John, 7 ; Wholesale and retail jeweller.
Lipetz, Lazarus, 7 ; Travelling jeweller.

DUFF STREET, DALRY ROAD.
Fedderman, L., 14 and 22 ; Waterproof garment manufacturer.

FOREST ROAD.
Goldfar, I., 4 ; Cigarette manufacturer and importer of foreign cigars and Turkish tobacco.

FOUNTAINBRIDGE, W.
Cornfield, S., 163 ; Waterproof garment manufacturer.

GARDNER'S CRESCENT.
Levenson, D., 5 ; Manager Caledonian Rubber Works.

EDINBURGH.

Commercial Directory of the Jews of Gt. Britain.

GEOFFREY STREET.
Harris, J., 5 ; Jeweller, clothier, and house-furnisher.

GEORGE STREET.
Davis, J., & Sons, 4 ; Stock and mortgage brokers.

GUTHRIE STREET.
Adler, A., 12 ; Select family baker.
Bernstein, S., 20 ; Tailor.

HIGH STREET.
Hyam, B., 124–6 ; Clothier and outfitter.
Michael Bros., 231 ; London pawnbroking sale rooms.
Michael Bros., 521 ; St. Giles pawnbroking sale rooms.

HILL PLACE.
Wolffe, M., 9 ; and 54, W. Richmond Street ; Wholesale and retail slipper manufacturer.

INFIRMARY STREET.
Langman, Myers, 8 ; Printer and publisher.
Myers, S., 4 ; Jeweller and watchmaker.

INGLISTON STREET.
Levy Bros., 6 ; Jewellers and watchmakers.

LAURISTON PLACE.
Lewis, A., & Co., 6 and 8 ; Wholesale and retail boot and slipper manufacturers.

LEITH WALK.
Camberg, L., 72, Brunswick Street ; Jeweller.
Franklin, B., 23, Albert Place; Manchester sale rooms.

EDINBURGH.

Commercial Directory of the Jews of Gt. Britain.

Freeman, E., & Son, 30, Elm Row; Drapers, clothiers, and general merchants.
Friedlansky, H., 283; The Glasgow sale room, dealer in watches, jewellery, and drapery.
Miller, C., 58, Elm Row; and 19, Dalry Road; Glasgow furnishing warehouse.
Stungo, M., 63, Elm Row; Manufacturer of waterproof garments

Lothian Street.

Benjamin, Max, 18; Clothier and draper.

Marchmont Road.

Esterson, S., 127; Watchmaker and jeweller.

Millerfield Place.

Eprile, R., 20; Wholesale and retail jeweller and watch dealer.

Moncrieff Terrace.

Bromberg, B., 12; Jeweller and watchmaker.

Montague Street.

Brown Bros., 24; and 31, Clerk Street, and at Methel, Fife; Jewellers and house-furnishers.
Luriansky, I., 7; Retail jeweller.
Shapera, M., 49; Watchmaker and jeweller.
Turiansky, B., 33; Jeweller and house-furnisher.

Newington Road.

Lindey, M. H., 26; Wholesale and retail watch dealer and jeweller. Est. 1870.

EDINBURGH.

Commercial Directory of the Jews of Gt. Britain.

николсон street.

*Geershon, Thos., 71; Branch: 57, Broad Street, Aberdeen. Hardware and fancy goods merchant and importer of foreign glass and china.

Goldston, D., 108; Carver and gilder and picture-frame manufacturer.

Hyman, Moses, 51A; Travelling jeweller.

Pleasance.

Braverman, Sol., 132; Jeweller.

Camberg, Gershon, 65; Jeweller.

Cohen, B., 14; Wholesale picture and show-card frame manufacturer.

Jablonsky, E., 126; Jeweller and draper.

Potter Row.

Cohen, L., 64; Jeweller and watchmaker.

Green, Jos., 8, Simpson's Court; Wholesale slipper manufacturer.

Preston Street, W.

Eprile, Nathan, 6; Watchmaker and jeweller.

Richmond Street.

Brown, L., 35 (N.); Watchmaker and jeweller.

Goldman, S., 25 (S.); Jeweller and draper.

Still, Jos., 23 (W.); Wholesale jeweller and purchaser of old gold and silver.

Salisbury Street.

Fineberg, J., 28; Boot and slipper manufacturer.

EDINBURGH.

Commercial Directory of the Jews of Gt. Britain.

St. Leonard's Street.
Alexander, Chas., 32 ; Jeweller and watchmaker.
Esterson, J., 47 ; Jeweller.

St. Patrick Square.
Priteca, Chas., 46 ; and at High Street, Kilsyth ; Draper, clothier, and boot merchant. Est. 1885.
Saltman, I., 48 ; Works : 65, Nicolson Street ; Waterproof garment manufacturer.

South Bridge.
Brown, P., 74 ; With Adair & Co. ; Master tailor.
Goldston, E. & M., 28 ; Wholesale and retail watch manufacturers and jewellers ; Importers of American, French, and German clocks.
Michael, J., 102 ; Wholesale jeweller and watch factor ; Agent for Swiss and American watches. Est. 1858.
Reis, Alphonse Louis, & Co., 36 ; and 10, Leith Street ; Jewellers and fancy merchants.

Thistle Street.
Bank, Leo, 43 ; Wholesale cigarette manufacturer.

Union Court, Richmond Place.
Festenstein, David, 3 ; Dealer in pictures and drapery.
Rev. Mr. Furst ; Minister Hebrew congregation.

LEITH.
Dresner, Ph., 61, Tolbooth Wynd ; Clothier and jeweller ; Branch : 18 and 19, Riddle's Close ; London and Glasgow Pawnbroking Co.
Hyman, Louis, 3, Tolbooth Wynd ; Clothier and jeweller.
Kerner, A., 60, Shore ; Seaman's outfitter.

GLASGOW.

Commercial Directory of the Jews of Gt. Britain.

ALBION STREET, N.
Frieze, Michael, 41 ; Master tailor.
Strump, Sol., 41 ; Master tailor.

ARGYLE STREET.
Friend, B., 230 ; Wholesale clothing manufacturer.
Goldberg, A., 20 (Arcade); Hairdresser and perfumer; and at 9 and 11, Gardner Street, Partick.
Jacobs, B. and N., 67 and 250 ; Clothiers.
Jacobs, Chas., 139 ; Clothier and outfitter.
Samuel, Henry, 7 ; Practical furrier.

BROOMIELAW.
Alexander, H., & Son, 120 and 138; Clothiers and foreign money exchange.
Dresdner, M., 214 and 192 ; Clothier and foreign money exchange.
Lizar & Son, 58 and 224 ; Exchange bank.

BRUNSWICK STREET.
Goldberg, I., 70 ; Master tailor.

BUCHANAN STREET.
Harris, A., 210 ; and at 143, Trongate, and 168, New City Road ; Cigar merchant.
Wolffe, Saml., 75 ; Works, 37, Vyse Street, Birmingham ; Manufacturing jeweller.

CANDLERIGGS.
Simons, Jacobs, & Co. ; Fruit brokers.

GLASGOW.

Commercial Directory of the Jews of Gt. Britain.

CLYDE STREET, GT.
Wexler, B., 6 ; Jeweller.

COCHRANE STREET.
Levi, Simon, 28 ; Master tailor.

COLLEGE STREET.
Clein, Louis, 47 ; General dealer.

COWCADDENS.
Isaacs, Isaac, 11, Maitland Street ; Master tailor.
Kann, M., 25, Findley Street ; Jeweller and general dealer.
Karnovski, S., 192 ; Watchmaker and jeweller.
Stern, Martin A., 124 ; Caledonian Clothing Co.

DERBY CRESCENT.
Cohen, Edmund, 5 ; Broker.

DUMBARTON ROAD.
Berenstein, Isidore, 120 ; Tobacconist.

DUNLOP STREET.
Cohen, Jac., 83 ; Wholesale clothing manufacturer.

GALLOWGATE.
Pinto, J., 28 ; Tailor and clothier.

GORDON SRREET.
Wolffe Bros., 46 ; Wholesale jewellers and watch manfrs.. And at 94, Vyse Street, Birmingham.

GLASGOW.

Commercial Directory of the Jews of Gt. Britain.

High Street.
Sagman, Morris, 285 ; Dealer in gold and silver.

Hope Street.
Schoenfield, A., & Co., 21 ; Iron and steel merchants.

John Street.
Cohen, A., 73 ; Clothier and jeweller.

Kingston.
Cohen, M., 64, Paterson Street; Wholesale clothing manufacturer.
Lissack, H., 64, Paterson Street; Wholesale mantle manufacturer.

Maxwell Street.
Phillips, B., 9 ; Tailor and mantle maker.
Phillips, Max, 9 ; Cigar importer.

Mitchell Street.
Lyons, Henry J., 43 ; Foreign agent and commission merchant.

Montrose Street.
Frankenburg, J., 18 ; Leather goods manufacturer.

Nelson Street.
Klahr, A., 46 ; Commission agent and remnant dealer.

New City Road.
Benson, H. L., 44 ; and at Douglas, I.O.M. ; Jeweller.
Jay, Alfred, 58 ; Clothier.

GLASGOW.

Commercial Directory of the Jews of Gt. Britain.

Louis, F., 245; The Western Furniture Co.; and at 16, Great Western Road.
Winter, H., 302; Clothier and outfitter.

Nile Street.
Cohen, E., & Co., 73 (W.); Lithographers and printers.
Samuels, Jac., 14 (E.); Master tailor.

Oswald Street.
Isaacs, Abm., 84; Master tailor.

Queen Street.
Radjes, L. A., 77; Boot agent.

Renfrew Street.
Ramus, Jos., 137; Fine art dealer.

Robertson Street.
Abrahams, N., 70; Master tailor.

Ropework Lane.
Phillips, Jos., 18; Skin and metal merchant.

Royal Exchange Place.
Sissel Bros., 7; Drysalters.

St. George's Road.
Pearlmann, M., & Co., 254; and 56, Jamaica Street; Photographer.
Sternstein, J., 364; Photographer.

GLASGOW.

Commercial Directory of the Jews of Gt. Britain.

St. Vincent Street.

Morris & Co., 204 ; Foreign merchants.

Dickie & Simons, 173 ; Solicitors.

Stockwell Street.

Bloom, Louis, 78 and 86 ; and 10, S. Place ; Wholesale picture-frame manufacturer.
Cohen, Morris, 140 ; Master tailor.
Davies, Abm., 5 (place) ; Master tailor.
Samuel, Hyman, 78 ; Master tailor.
Stern, S., 21 ; Watchmaker and jeweller.

Trongate.

Freedman, E., 163 ; Clothier and outfitter.

Gershon, I., 139 ; Wholesale clothier.

Union Street.

Abrahams, S., Warerooms, 68-70 ; Union Furniture Co. Cabinet Works, 120-130, Waterloo Street.

Levy, Victor, & Co., 40 ; Watch manufacturers and wholesale jewellers. And 36, Northampton Street, Birmingham.

Woodside Road, N.

Aaronson, Jac., 81 and 85 ; Clothier and furnisher.

South Side.

Adelphi Street.

Hyman, E., 44 ; Wholesale picture and show-card frame manufacturer and importer of mouldings, and glass merchant.

GLASGOW.

Commercial Directory of the Jews of Gt. Britain.

APSLEY PLACE.

Myers, George D., 5 ; Importer of tobacconists' goods.

CROWN STREET.

Abrahamson, I., 157 ; Jeweller and general dealer.
Blumenthal M., 203 ; Master tailor.
Grundland, Alfred, 157 ; Cigarette maker.
Orveigh, P., 13 ; Master tailor.

CUMEERLAND STREET.

Isaacs, E., 270 ; Draper and general dealer.
Rosenbloom, H., 198 ; General dealer.

DUNMORE STREET.

Barnett, A., 36 ; Family butcher and poulterer ; Agent for Anchor Line S. S. Co.
Bridge, Isaac (Rev.), 31 ; Minister S. S. Synagogue ; Bookseller.
Naftalin, A., 11 and 13 ; Vienna and German baker and family grocer.

FLORENCE STREET.

Blumberg, J., 31 ; General dealer.
Riffkin, Jos., 131 ; Jeweller and draper.
Schmulovitz, J., 39 ; General dealer.

GOVAN STREET.

Adler, S. H., 174 ; Draper and general dealer.

Fisher, J., 5 ; Wholesale picture and show-card frame manufacturer.

Goldston, M., 14 ; Baker, foreign grocer, and provision merchant.

Lurie, Saml., 30 ; Butcher and poulterer.

Hospital Street.

Cohen, A., 136 ; Draper and general dealer.

Main Street.

Lipshitz, B., 18 ; Vienna and German bread factory and family grocer.

Louis, Benj., 16 ; Master tailor.

Markson, I., 80 ; Jeweller.

Marzynski, M., 129 ; and cor. Hope and Main, Anderston ; Clothier and outfitter.

Myers, Israel, 111 ; Master tailor.

Riffkin, A., 151 ; Wholesale and retail picture and show-card frame manufacturer and glass merchant.

Rudom, J., 16 ; Jeweller.

Norfolk Street.

Levy, J., 37 ; Wholesale and retail picture and show-card frame manufacturer and glass merchant.

Oxford Street.

Elstine, N., 114 ; Master tailor.

Solomon, M., 46 ; Master tailor.

GLASGOW.

Commercial Directory of the Jews of Gt. Britain.

PORTLAND STREET, S.

Jacobs, Hyman, 99 ; Master tailor.
Posner, J., 16 ; Wholesale clothier.

ROSE STREET.

Carnovski, M., 14 ; Jeweller and general dealer.
Cohen, David, 14 ; General dealer.
Simons, D., 14 ; Master tailor.

RUTHERGLEN ROAD.

Bernstein, Mrs., & Son, 17 ; Drapers.
Bovilsky, Jac., 139 ; Cigarette maker.
Dumbrovsky, J., 31 ; Draper and general dealer.
Hyman, Louis, 22 ; Watchmaker and jeweller.
Jacobs, A., 139 ; Master tailor for P. Paisley.
Joels, Emanuel, 139.
Josephthall, A. J., 14 ; General dealer.
Pollock, S., 35 ; Wholesale and retail picture-frame manufacturer.
Samuel, J., 20 ; Picture and show-card frame manfr.

SALISBURY STREET.

Pinkus, Sol., 6 ; Tailor and clothier.

THISTLE STREET.

Barnett, Simon, 130 ; Draper and general dealer.

WELLINGTON STREET, S.

Margolyes, S., 189 ; Jeweller.

GLASGOW.

Commercial Directory of the Jews of Gt. Britain.

KILWINNING.

Levy, A. ; General dealer.

POLLOKSHIELDS.

Kramrisch, J., 77, Forth.
Rev. Mr. Phillips ; Minister Hebrew congregation.

WALES.

ABERDARE.

Commercial Directory of the Jews of Gt. Britain.

BUTE STREET.
Fine, Jac., 11 and 12; Pawnbroker, jeweller, and clothier.
Price, Jac., 57; House-furnisher.

CANON STREET.
Cohen, B., 13; Watchmaker and jeweller.
Lazarus, Lewis, 42; House-furnisher.

CARDIFF STREET.
Jacobs, M., 14; Pawnbroker and clothier.

ABERAMAN.

CARDIFF STREET.
Jacobs, Wm., 141A; House-furnisher.
Mendelsohn, B., 91A; Watchmaker and jeweller.

LEWIS STREET.
Jacobs, Saml. A., 47, 48; Pawnbroker and outfitter.

ABERGAVENNY.

FROGMORE STREET.
Fine, Marks, 35; Pawnbroker and jeweller.

WALES.

Commercial Directory of the Jews of Gt. Britain.

BLANARVON.

Albert Street.

Jacobs, R., & Co., 9; Pawnbrokers, outfitters, and jewellers.

Broad Street.

Robinson, J., 78, 79; Complete house-furnisher and jeweller.

BRYNMAWR.

Bailey Street.

Abrahams, N., 26, 27; House-furnisher.
Brest, I., 24; House-furnisher.
Isaacs, Isaac; Pawnbroker.
Solomon, M., 30, 31; House-furnisher.

Beaufort Street.

Edlit, A., 34; House-furnisher.
Isaacs, B., 41; Pawnbroker.

Nantyglo.

Norvick & Norvick, Garn; Outfitters, jewellers, and boot merchants.
Weiner, Goodman, Garn; Ironmonger.

CARDIFF.

Adam Street.

Cohen, Louis, 42; House-furnisher and auctioneer. Islington, London.

WALES.

Commercial Directory of the Jews of Gt. Britain.

BRIDGE STREET.

Goldman, Hyman, 1, Wellington Terrace; Insurance broker and general commission agent.

Goldman, S., 55; Glass dealer.

Shatz, B.; Wholesale and retail picture-frame and looking-glass manufacturer.

BUTE STREET.

Barnett, Louis, & Son, 19 and 49; and 6 and 7, Caroline Street; Pawnbrokers and jewellers.

Jacobs, Barnett, 41, 42; and 1, Herbert Street; Pawnbroker, jeweller, and outfitter.

Phillips, Israel, 13; Pawnbroker and jeweller.

Shapiro, S., 293; Picture-frame maker.

BUTE TERRACE.

Lewis, A., 30; Pawnbroker and clothier.

Pollock, W., 18; House-furnisher and general dealer.

CANTON.

Cohen, Jos., 84, Cowbridge Road; Pawnbroker, clothier, and jeweller.

Epstein, E., 66, Tudor Road; Pawnbroker and clothier.

Levene, H., Cowbridge Road; Pawnbroker, clothier, and jeweller.

Solomon, J., 293, Cowbridge Road; Bespoke tailor and tailor for the trade.

CAROLINE STREET.

Phillips, Sol., 43; Pawnbroker and jeweller.

WALES.

Commercial Directory of the Jews of Gt. Britain.

CATHAYS.

Cohen, H., 1, Mundy Place; Pawnbroker, clothier, and jeweller.

Levene, Wolfe, 94, Woodville Road; and 86, Salisbury Road; Pawnbroker, clothier, and jeweller.

DOCKS.

Isaacs, H., 152, Bute Road; Outfitter, hatter, etc.

Joseph, S. W., 198, Bute Street; and 53, George Street; Jeweller, watchmaker, and clothier.

Michaelson, J., 47 and 50, James Street; Pawnbroker.

Samuel S., 140; Outfitter.

ELDON STREET.

Baron, Sol., 107; Master tailor.

Bloom, A., 73; Master tailor.

Cohen, Wolfe, 49; Master tailor.

Marx, Myer, 101; Master tailor.

HAYS.

Samuel, L.; House-furnisher.

GRANGE.

Abrahamson, C., 6, Bromsgrove Street; Pawnbroker.

Finsburg, L., 82–84, Holmesdale Street; Pawnbroker.

NELSON TERRACE.

Barnett, Annetta, 9; Pawnbroker, jeweller, and outfitter.

Cohen, P., 5; Glass merchant.

NEW STREET.

Morris, J.; Fruit dealer.

WALES.

Commercial Directory of the Jews of Gt. Britain.

Park Street.

Wasserzug, D., B.A. (Rev.) ; Minister Cardiff Hebrew congregation.

Fishman, Barnett, 8 ; House-furnisher.

Quay Street.

Joseph, Louis, 19 ; Financial agent.

Queen Street.

Bomash, T. S., 19 ; Jeweller and pawnbroker.

Cohen Bros., 104 ; and 48, Clifton Street ; Complete house-furnishers.

Lewis, J., 85 ; Complete house-furnisher.

Roath.

Barnett, Isabella, 24, B'way ; Jeweller and tobacconist.

Fligelstone, M. ; Pawnbroker and jeweller.

Freedman, J., 2, Constellation Street ; Pawnbroker.

Freydberg, F., 44, System Street ; Pawnbroker.

Joseph, A. ; Pawnbroker and jeweller.

Lewis, M., 67, Castle Road ; Pawnbroker and jeweller.

Shibko, A., 76, B'way ; Pawnbroker and jeweller.

St. Mary Street.

Phillips, H. W., 33 ; Clothier and outfitter.

Phillips, P. & Co., 43 ; and 3, Caroline Street ; The Model Clothing Co.

Saltmead.

Cossick, L., 37, Clare Road ; Tailor and outfitter.

WALES.

Commercial Directory of the Jews of Gt. Britain.

SPLOTLAND.

Abrahamson, Joshua, 17, Splott Road; Pawnbroker and clothier.

Fine, Morris, 33, Clifton Street; Pawnbroker, jeweller, and clothier.

Goldman, Jacob, 66, Railway Street; Complete house-furnisher.

Reed, Leon, 56, Railway Street; Pawnbroker and outfitter.

Samuel, S., 2, Splott Road; Watchmaker and jeweller.

TUDOR ROAD.

Cohen, Michael, 16; Master tailor.

Jacobius, Marcus, 58; Hairdresser and tobacconist.

WOOD STREET.

Isaacs, A., 38; Pawnbroker and clothier.

Jacobs, Elias, 29; Master tailor.

Minski, L. (Rev.), 31; Teacher of Hebrew and religion.

Weston, Henry, 49–51; Furnisher and tailor.

WORKING STREET.

Edells, A. H., 23; Looking-glass manufacturer.

Levene, L., 19; Wholesale and retail picture and show-card frame manufacturer.

PENARTH.

Harris, Hyman, 85, Glebe Street; Pawnbroker, outfitter, watchmaker, and jeweller. Est. 1882.

WALES.

Commercial Directory of the Jews of Gt. Britain.

DOWLAIS.

High Street.

Freedman, A. I., 76 and 76A, Victoria Buildings; Pawnbroker, jeweller, and outfitter.
Freedman, Harris, 149; Pawnbroker and outfitter.
Harris Bros., 80; Complete house-furnishers.
Levinsohn, Marcus, 100; General house-furnisher.

Horse Street.

Isaacs, Harris; Pawnbroker and outfitter.

Union Street.

Freedman, G.; House-furnisher.
Gittlesohn, H., cor. Brecon and Union; Pawnbroker and outfitter.
Hyman, J. H., 17; Watchmaker and Jeweller.

EBBW VALE.

Commercial Street.

Goldblatt, C., 29; Cabinet and picture-frame manfr.
Lyons, Marks J. S.; Pawnbroker, outfitter, and jeweller. Also at "Star Supply," Market Street.

Victoria Road.

Cohen, A., & Co., 16; Jewellers, furnishers, and clothiers.
Simons, M., 47; Complete house-furnisher.

WALES.

Commercial Directory of the Jews of Gt. Britain.

MERTHYR.

BETHSEDA STREET.

Bernstein, E., 46 ; House-furnisher.
Goodman, Moses, 3 and 6, Victoria Street; Pawnbroker.
Isaacs, C., 13 ; Pawnbroker and clothier.

BRECON ROAD.

Levi, I. R., 21 ; Clothier.

LOWER HIGH STREET.

Prag, Julius, 16 and 17 ; Pawnbroker, jeweller, and furniture dealer.

LOWER THOMAS STREET.

Joseph, A., 85 ; Jeweller and old gold and silver dealer.

PENYDARREN.

PICTON STREET.

Freedman, Lewis ; Pawnbroker, jeweller, clothier, and furniture dealer. Est. 1850.
Goodman, J., 36 ; Pawnbroker.

PONTMORLAIS.

Cohen, W. R., 93 ; Pawnbroker and general dealer.

TEMPERANCE STREET.

Isaacs, A., 10 ; Jeweller.
Karnofsky, J. I., 7 ; Jeweller and general dealer.

UNION STREET.

Abelson, A. (Rev.) ; Reader Merthyr Hebrew congregation.

WALES.

Commercial Directory of the Jews of Gt. Britain.

VICTORIA STREET.

Cohen, B., 11A; Clothier.
Jacobs, A. B., 21; Pawnbroker, clothier, etc.
Lazarus, E., 5; Furniture dealer.
Mendelsohn, P., 12; Watchmaker and jeweller.

MOUNT ASH.

DUFFERIN STREET.

Levinson, B., 53; Boot and shoe merchant and general dealer.
Levinson, L., 42; Complete house-furnisher.

FRWYD CRESCENT.

Barnett, Harris, 5; Pawnbroker, jeweller, and clothier.

OXFORD STREET.

Fine, J., 78; Furniture dealer, etc.

NEW TREDEGAR.

Harris, M., Elliots-town; Clothier and boot and shoe dealer.
Simons, M., Elliots-town; Complete house-furnisher.

PONTLOTTYN.

Goldenson, Em., 7, Bridge Street; Outfitter and general dealer.
Mendelsohn, W., 44, Merchant Street; Watchmaker and jeweller.

WALES.

Commercial Directory of the Jews of Gt. Britain.

RHYNNEY.

Fine, Tobias & Son, 94, High Street; and Lawn Terrace and Pontlottyn; Pawnbrokers, outfitters, jewellers, furnishers, and boot merchants.

PONTYPOOL.

ALBION ROAD.

Grosenor, S., 31; Picture-frame and general dealer.

GEORGE STREET.

Harris, B.; Clothier and boot dealer; also at Abercarn, Risca, and Ebbw Vale.
Kremer, S., 53; Furnisher and picture-frame dealer.

NICOLAS STREET.

Orman, N. A., 7; Draper and general dealer.
Robin, S., 8; Picture and general dealer.

PONTNEWYNYDD.

Dowson, Samuel I., 7, Hill Street; Picture-frames, outfitter, and furnisher.

RHONDDA VALLEY.

FERNDALE.

Cohen, Eli, 23, Duffryn Street; Complete house-furnisher.
Joseph, Eli, 61, Duffryn Street; Pawnbroker, jeweller, and clothier.
Love, J., 34, Lake Street; Complete house-furnisher.
Shibko, A., 16 and 50, Strand; Outfitter, jeweller, and boot merchant.

WALES.

Commercial Directory of the Jews of Gt. Britain.

PEN-Y-GRAIG.

Freedman, M., Pen-y-graig Road ; Clothier.
Pollack, L. ; Pawnbroker, jeweller, and clothier.

PENTRE.

Cohen, I., 30, Llewelyn Street ; Complete house-furnisher.
Cohen, Israel, 161, Ystrad Road ; Pawnbroker and clothier.
Lorie, M., 24, Ystrad Road ; Pawnbroker, jeweller, and outfitter.

PONTYPRIDD.

Freedman, M. ; Pawnbroker, jeweller, and clothier.
Ginsberg, A. ; Glass dealer.
Malitz, M. ; Watchmaker and jeweller.
Marks, F. ; Wall-paper dealer.
Posnor, J. (Rev.) ; Reader Hebrew congregation.
Rosenbloom, L. ; Furniture and general dealer.

PORTH.

Isaacs, J., 14, Harness Street ; Pawnbroker and general dealer.

TON-Y-PANDY.

Ash, H ; Watchmaker, jeweller, and dealer in musical instruments and fancy goods.
Green, Em. ; Pawnbroker, jeweller, and clothier.
Robinson, S. ; Furniture dealer and clothier.
Stone, M., Pandy Square ; House-furnisher and clothier.

WALES.

Commercial Directory of the Jews of Gt. Britain.

Treharris.

Joseph, Myer, 1, John Street; Pawnbroker, jeweller, and clothier.

Shapira, I., 14, Brynteg Terrace; Watchmaker and jeweller.

Treherbert.

Fine, Marks, 20 and 21, Dunraven Street; Pawnbroker, outfitter, and jeweller.

Treorky.

Barons', High Street; Furniture dealers and clothiers.

Love, B., Liverpool House, High Street; Complete house-furnisher.

Troedyrhiew.

Fine, S. W., 27, Yew Street; and 10 and 11, Poplar Street; Furnisher, draper, and jeweller.

SWANSEA.

Belle Vue.

Seline, I.; Financier.

Seline; Solicitor.

Miron, J. (Rev.); Reader Hebrew congregation.

Castle Street.

Freedman, B.; Musical instruments.

Craddoc Street.

Goldman; Jeweller.

Owen, F. D.; Dental surgeon. Swansea and Cardiff.

WALES.

Commercial Directory of the Jews of Gt. Britain.

Dynevor Place.
Barnett, Sol., 11 ; Auctioneer, mortgage broker, and financier.

Heathfield Street.
Barnett, Henry, 6 ; Clothier, etc.

High Street.
Goldberg ; Pawnbroker and jeweller.
Lyons, Abm., 25 ; and 64, Lower Oxford Street ; Pawnbroker, jeweller, and clothier.
Lyons, S., 155 ; Pawnbroker, outfitter, and jeweller.

Llangfallach.
Levy, D. ; Pawnbroker.

Northampton Place.
Goldberg ; Shipowner.

Oxford Street.
Barnett, D., 63 ; Cabinet maker and furnisher.
Mendelson, P., 113 (lower) ; Pawnbroker, jeweller, and clothier.

Russell Street.
Phillips ; Auctioneer.

St. Helen's Road.
Goodman, G. ; Financier.

Scyberfach.
Jacobs ; Pawnbroker and clothier.
Silverman, M. ; Pawnbroker and clothier.

WALES.

Commercial Directory of the Jews of Gt. Britain.

Walter's Road.
Marks ; Financier.

Morriston.
Freedman, A. ; Pawnbroker, jeweller, and clothier.

Neath.
Nathan, Mrs. ; Pawnbroker, clothier, etc.
Samuels ; Pawnbroker, clothier, etc.

TREDEGAR.

Harris, Herman ; Pawnbroker, outfitter, and boot merchant.

Bridge Street.
Bernstein, L., 28 ; Outfitter and hatter.
Samuel, P., 35 ; Pawnbroker and boot dealer.

Church Street.
Rosenbaum, S., 55 ; Pawnbroker and clothier.
Wolfson, S., 31 and 15 ; Pawnbroker and outfitter.

Commercial Road.
Zeffert, I., 80 ; Wholesale and retail tobacconist and fancy repository.

Market Street.
Davidson, M., 27 ; Pawnbroker and jeweller.

Queen Street.
Harris, Louis S., 87 ; Pawnbroker and clothier.

www.ingramcontent.com/pod-product-compliance
Lightning Source LLC
Chambersburg PA
CBHW032006230426
43672CB00010B/2273